The Saxon Age

The Saxon Age
commentaries of an era

A F Scott

179

 CROOM HELM LONDON

© 1979 Scott and Finlay Ltd
Croom Helm Ltd, 2-10 St John's Road, London SW11

British Library Cataloguing in Publication Data
Scott, Arthur Finley
    The Saxon age.
    1. Civilization, Anglo-Saxon
    I. Title
    942.01   DA152.2
    ISBN 0-85664-905-8

Printed in Great Britain by
Biddles Ltd, Guildford, Surrey

Contents

List of Illustrations

The author and publisher acknowledge with thanks permission to reproduce the illustrations listed below.

TO MAUREEN AND WALTER

Acknowledgements

The author and publishers are grateful to the authorities named for permission to use copyright material. Furthermore, the publishers have tried to trace the owners of all copyright material and apologise for any omissions. Should these be made known to us proper acknowledgements will be made in future editions.

Eyre Methuen, Ltd, for passages from *English Historical Documents*, Volume I, edited by Dorothy Whitelock, and for two passages translated by Margaret Ashdown.

J.M. Dent and Sons, Ltd, for an extract from *Anglo-Saxon Chronicle*, translated by G.N. Garmonsway, and for 'Nine Herbs Charm' from *Anglo-Saxon Poetry*, translated by R.K. Gordon.

Longman Group, Ltd, for a passage from *England before the Norman Conquest*, by R.W. Chambers (University of London, Intermediate source-books of History No. VIII.

Oxford University Press for a passage from *The Life of King Edward the Confessor*, edited and translated by Frank Barlow.

Routledge and Kegan Paul, Ltd, for the poems 'Senility', 'The Hermit's Hut' (revised translation), the prose 'St Brendan's Vision of Hell' from *A Celtic Miscellany*, translated by Kenneth Hurlstone Jackson.

Penguin Books, Ltd, for an extract from 'The Funeral of Scyld Shefing', from *Beowulf*, p. 49, lines 26-52, Gnomic Verses, pp. 88-9, lines 71-99, 'The Ruin', pp. 30-1, lines 1-49, from *The Earliest English Poems*, translated by Michael Alexander; and for passages from Bede, *A History of the English Church and People*, translated by Leo Sherley-Price, pp. 68-70 and pp. 146-7.

The Present State of Britain, 731

At the present time, the Picts have a treaty of peace with the English, and are glad to be united in Catholic peace and truth to the universal Church. The Scots who are living in Britain are content with their own territories, and do not contemplate any raids or stratagems against the English. The Britons for the most part have a national hatred for the English, and uphold their own bad customs against the true Easter of the Catholic Church; however, they are opposed by the power of God and man alike, and are powerless to obtain what they want. For, although in part they are independent, they have been brought in part under subjection to the English.

As such peace and prosperity prevail in these days, many of the Northumbrians, both noble and simple, together with their children, have laid aside their weapons, preferring to receive the tonsure and take monastic vows rather than study the arts of war. What the result of this will be the future will show.

This, then, is the present state of all Britain, about two hundred and eighty-five years after the coming of the English to Britain, but seven hundred and thirty-one years since our Lord's Incarnation. May the world rejoice under his eternal rule, and Britain glory in his Faith! *Let the multitude of isles be glad thereof, and give thanks at the remembrance of his holiness!* — Bede, from *Historia Ecclesiastica Gentis Anglorum*, translated by Leo Sherley-Price.

1 Royalty

This Comment on Geoffrey of Monmouth Was Made c.1170, Praising King Arthur

What place is there within the bounds of the empire of Christendom to which the winged praise of Arthur the Briton has not extended? Who is there, I ask, who does not speak of Arthur the Briton, since he is but little less known to the peoples of Asia than to the Bretons, as we are informed by our palmers who return from the countries of the East? The Eastern peoples speak of him as do the Western, though separated by the breadth of the whole earth. Egypt speaks of him, and the Bosphorus is not silent. Rome, queen of cities, sings his deeds, and his wars are not unknown to her former rival Carthage, Antioch, Armenia and Palestine celebrate his feats — from Geoffrey Ashe (ed.), *The Quest for Arthur's Britain*.

Maelgwn, Western King, 'Dragon of the Island', c. 520-551

His story of one who had 'deprived many tyrants of their kingdoms and their lives' is told by Gildas.

In the first years of your youth, you crushed the king your uncle and his bravest troops with fire and spear and sword. When your dream of violent rule was realised, your longing for the right road pulled you back, perhaps because your sins then bit your conscience; day and night you pondered . . . the life of the monks, and then publicly proclaimed that you would vow yourself a monk for ever, before God Almighty, in the sight of the angels and of men with no thought of going back on your promise.

You seemed suddenly to have broken through the vast nets that normally entangle fat bulls of your kind, the chains of royal power, of gold and silver, and, what matters more, of your own over-weening will . . . when you came to the cave of the saints. How great the joy of the

11

1. A Saxon king and his witan, the national council in Anglo-Saxon times, reach the verdict of guilty.

church our mother, if the Enemy of all mankind . . . had not snatched you from the Lord's fold . . . with no very vigorous resistance on your part . . . to make you a wolf like himself. For the rejoicing at your conversion to the good fruit was as great as the grief . . . at your reversion to your frightful vomit. Your excited ears heard no more the praises of God, sung by the gentle voices of Christ's soldiers, nor the melodious chanting of the church, but your own empty praises, shouted by lying thieves shrieking in frenzy — Gildas, *De Exicidio et Conquestu Britanniae*. From John Morris, *The Age of Arthur*.

Urien of Rheged, King of Cumbria, Was Murdered by the English, *c*. 573, Off the Northumbrian Coast

His head was carried away by his cousin.

A head I carry, close to my side,
Head of Urien, generous leader of hosts,
And on his white breast, a black carrion crow.
A head I carry . . .
Alive he was a refuge for the old.
A head I carry . . .
Whose war-bands patrolled vast territories
The Head of much-sung Urien, whose fame is far scattered.
A head I hold up which once sustained me . . .
My arm is numb, my body trembles,
My heart breaks;
This head I cherish formerly cherished me.

Nennius, *Historia Britonum.*

Grant by Hlothhere, King of Kent, to Abbot Brihtwold of Land in Thanet, 679

In the name of our Lord and Saviour Jesus Christ. I, Hlothhere, king of the people of Kent, grant for the relief of my soul land in Thanet which is called *Westanae* to you, Brihtwold, and to your monastery, with everything belonging to it, fields, pastures, marshes, small woods, fens, fisheries, with everything, as has been said, belonging to that same land. As it has been owned hitherto, by the well-known boundaries indicated by me and my reeves, we confer it in the same way to you and your monastery. May you hold and possess it, and your successors maintain it for ever. May it not be contradicted by anyone. With the consent of Archbishop Theodore and Eadric, my brother's son, and also of all the leading men, as it has been granted to you, hold it thus, you and your successors. May whoever attempts to contravene this donation be cut off from all Christendom, and debarred from the body and blood of our Lord Jesus Christ, this charter of donation remaining nevertheless in its firmness. And I have both formed the sign of the Cross for its confirmation with my own hand and asked witnesses to subscribe.

Done in the city of Reculver, in the month of May, the seventh indiction . . . Sign of the hand of King Hlothhere, the donor — *English Historical Documents*, Vol. I.

The Legend of King Alfred

. . . as we read in the life of the holy father St Neot, he was long concealed in the dwelling of one of his own cowherds.

It happened one day that the country-woman the wife of this cowherd, was baking some cakes for food, while the king was sitting before the fire, and repairing his bow and arrows and instruments of war. When the unlucky woman saw that the cakes which she had placed on the fire were burning, she ran up in great haste and removed them, and scolded our invincible king after this fashion — 'Look, man, the cakes are burning, and you do not take the trouble to turn them; when the time for eating them comes, then you are active enough' — Asser, *Life of King Alfred*, translated by L.C. Jane.

Alfred, 849-901, King of the West Saxons

As he advanced through the years of infancy and youth, his form appeared more comely than that of his brothers; in look, in speech and in manner, he was more graceful than they.

Though established in royal power, the king was wounded by the nails of many tribulations. From his twentieth to his forty-fifth year (in which he now is) he has been troubled incessantly by the severe visitation of an unknown disease; never an hour passes but he either suffers

2. Silver penny of King Offa of Mercia struck at Canterbury *c*. 790 by a moneyer called Ibba. As Ralph Arnold says, this silver penny set the pattern for English coinage over the next 500 years.

from it, or is nearly desperate from fear of it — Asser, Bishop of Sherbourne, *Life of Alfred.*

King Alfred, in his Translation of Boethius, Added This on Kingship

This, then [he wrote], is a king's material and his tools for ruling with, that he have his land fully manned. He must have men who pray, and soldiers and workmen. Lo, you know that without these tools no king can reveal his skill. Also, this is his material, which he must have for those tools — sustenance for those three orders; and their sustenance consists in land to live on, and gifts, and weapons, and food, and ale, and clothes, and whatever else those three orders require — from King Alfred's translation of the *De Consolatione Philosophiae* of Boethius.

How a Certain Boy, Guthfrith, Was Made King, 883

Following the Danish settlement of 876 in the north, it is interesting to see how the appointment of a Christian Danish king owed it to the Church.

At that time [883] St Cuthbert appeared by night to the holy abbot of Carlisle, whose name was Eadred, firmly enjoining him as follows: 'Go', he said, 'across the Tyne to the army of the Danes, and say to them that, if they will obey me, they are to point out to you a certain boy, Guthfrith, Hardacnut's son, by name, a purchased slave of a certain widow, and you and the whole army are to give in the early morning the price for him to the widow [at Whittington]; and give the afore-said price at the third hour, and at the sixth hour lead him before the whole multitude, that they may elect him king. And at the ninth hour lead him with the whole army on to the hill which is called 'Oswiu's down', and there place on his right arm a gold armlet, and thus they all may appoint him as king. Also say to him, when he has been made king, that he is to give me the whole territory between the Tyne and the Wear; and whoever shall flee to me, whether on account of homicide, or or any other necessity; is to have sanctuary for 37 days and nights.'

Resolved as a result of this vision, and strengthened by the reason-able command of the blessed confessor, the holy abbot confidently hastened to the barbarian army; and being honourably received by it, he faithfully carried out in order what had been enjoined on him. For he both found and redeemed the boy, and made him king by the great goodwill of the whole multitude, receiving the land and right of sanctu-ary. Then Bishop Eardwulf brought to the army and to the hill the body of St Cuthbert, and over it the king himself and the whole army swore peace and fidelity, for as long as they lived; and they kept this oath well — from the anonymous *History of St Cuthbert*, edited by T. Arnold, *Symeonis Monachii Opera Omnia*, translated by Dorothy Whitelock, *English Historical Documents*, Vol. I.

King Aethelstan, 924-939

Chap. 134: He was affable and kind to the servants of God, pleasant and courteous to the laymen, serious, out of regard for his majesty, to the magnates, kind and moderate to the lesser folk, out of condescension for their poverty, putting aside the pride of kingship. He was, as we have learnt, not beyond what is becoming in stature, and slender in body; his hair, as we have ourselves seen from his relics, flaxen, beautifully mingled with gold threads. He was much beloved by his subjects, out of admiration of his courage and humility, but like a thunderbolt to rebels by his invincible steadfastness — William of Malmesbury, *The Deeds of the English Kings, English Historical Documents*, Vol. I.

Aethelstan Deserts the Christian Faith and Restores Idolatry, 925

Aethelstan, king of the English, joined in matrimony with great ceremony his sister Eadgyth with Sihtric, king of the Northumbrians, sprung from the Danish race; and he gave up the heathen religion for the love of the maiden and received the faith of Christ. But not long afterwards he cast off the blessed maiden and, deserting his Christianity, restored the worship of idols, and after a short while ended his life miserably as an apostate. Accordingly the holy maiden, having preserved her chastity, remained strong in good works to the end of her life, at Polesworth, in fasts and in vigils, in prayers and in zeal for almsgiving. She departed after the passage of a praiseworthy life from this world on 15 July, at this same place, where to this day divine miracles do not cease to be performed — Roger of Wendover, *Flores Historiarum*, translated by Dorothy Whitelock, *English Historical Documents*, Vol. I.

Royal Gifts

Hugh the Great, Duke of the Franks married the sister of King Aethelstan. When he sent his request for this English princess, he chose his embassy and gifts with impressive skill. Baldwin, Count of Flanders, whose wife was Aethelstan's aunt, led the party, and before nobles at Abingdon offered these splendid gifts:

. . . perfumes such as had never before been seen in England; jewellery, especially of emeralds, in whose greenness the reflected sun lit up the eyes of the bystanders with a pleasing light; many fleet horses, with trappings, 'champing', as Maro [Virgil] says, 'on bits of ruddy gold'; a vase of onyx, carved with such subtle engravers' art that the corn fields seemed really to wave, the vines ready to bud, the forms of the men really to move, and so clear and polished that it reflected like a mirror the faces of the onlookers; the sword of Constantine the Great, on which could be read the name of the ancient owner in letters of gold; on the pommel also, above thick plates of gold, you could see an iron nail fixed, one of the four which the Jewish faction prepared for the crucifixion of our Lord's body; the spear of Charles the Great . . . said to be the same which, driven by the hand of the centurion into our Lord's side, opened up the gash of that precious wound Paradise for wretched mortals . . . — William of Malmesbury, *Gesta Regum Anglo-rum*.

King Edgar, 959-975

i. 959. In this year King Eadwig died and his brother Edgar succeeded to the kingdom; in his days things improved greatly, and God granted him that he lived in peace as long as he lived; and, as was necessary for him, he laboured zealously for this; he exalted God's praise far and wide, and loved God's law; and he improved the peace of the people more than the kings who were before him in the memory of man.

ii. 973. In this year, Edgar was consecrated king on Whit Sunday at Bath in the thirteenth year after his accession, and when he was twenty-nine years old. Soon after this, the king led all his fleet to Chester, and there six kings came to him to make their submission, and pledged themselves to be his fellow workers by sea and land — *Anglo-Saxon Chronicle, English Historical Documents*, Vol. I.

Kenneth, King of the Scots, to Meet King Edgar Every Year at Festivals, 975, and So for Their Successors

Then he [King Edgar] ordered a new coinage to be made throughout the whole of England, because the old was so debased by the crime of clippers that a penny hardly weighed a half-penny on the scales. About the same time, Bishop Ælfsige and Earl Eadwulf conducted Kenneth, king of the Scots, to King Edgar; and when they had brought him to the king, he was given great gifts by the royal munificence; among which the king bestowed on him a hundred ounces of the purest gold, with many adornments of silk and rings with precious stones. He gave besides to the same king all the land which is called Lothian in the native language, on this condition, that every year at the principal festivals, when the king and his successors wore their crowns, they (the king of the Scots) should come to the court and joyfully celebrate the feast with the rest of the nobles of the kingdom. Moreover, the king gave him many residences on the way, so that he and his successors coming to the festival and returning thence could be lodged there, and these remained in the power of the kings of the Scots until the time of King Henry the Second — Roger of Wendover, *Flores Historiarum*, translated by Dorothy Whitelock, *English Historical Documents*, Vol. I.

King Ethelred II, 978-1016

King Ethelred, the illustrious atheling, was consecrated to the supreme dignity of the kingdom by the apostolic man Dunstan and his co-apostle Oswald, and there was great rejoicing at his consecration. For he was young in years, graceful in manners, beautiful in face and comely in appearance . . . During his reign the abominable Danes came to the kingdom of the English, and laying waste and burning everything, did not spare men, but, glorying in flashing blades and poisoned arrows, armed themselves in bronze helmets, in which they fought and were wont to terrify beholders — *Life of St Oswald, English Historical Documents*, Vol. I.

King Swein

i. 1013. Then King Swein turned from there to Wallingford, and so West across the Thames to Bath, where he stayed with his army. Then Ealdorman Aethelmar came there, and with him the western thegns, and all submitted to Swein, and they gave him hostages. When he had fared thus, he then turned northwards to his ships, and all the nation regarded him as full king.

ii. 1014. In this year Swein ended his days at Candlemas, on 3 February, and then all the fleet elected Cnut king. Then all the councillors who were in England, ecclesiastical and lay, determined to send for King Ethelred, and they said that no lord was dearer to them than their

natural lord, if he would govern them more justly than he did before —
Anglo-Saxon Chronicle, English Historical Documents, Vol. I.

Edmund Ironside

1016. Then it happened that King Ethelred died before the ships
arrived. He ended his days on St George's day, and he had held his
kingdom with great toil and difficulties as long as his life lasted. And
after his death, all the councillors who were in London and the citizens
chose Edmund as king and he stoutly defended his kingdom while his
life lasted — *Anglo-Saxon Chronicle, English Historical Documents*,
Vol. I.

King Cnut, 1016—1035

Cnut reigned for twenty years. He died at Shaftesbury and was buried
at Winchester in the Old Monastery. A few facts about his reign should
be briefly told, for never before him was there a king in England of
such greatness. For he was lord of all Denmark, all England, all Norway
and at the same time of Scotland. Over and above the number of wars
in which he was so glorious, he did three handsome and magnificent
acts. Firstly he married his daughter [Gunhild] to the Roman Emperor
[Henry III] with indescribable riches. Secondly on his path to Rome
[1031] he paid money and reduced by as much as a half all those evil
exactions called tolls and portages on the road which leads to Rome
through France. Thirdly, at the very summit of his power, he ordered
his throne to be set on the seaside when the tide was rising. He addressed
the mounting waters, 'You are under my sway as is the land on which is
my throne and there has never been anyone who has resisted my rule
without being punished. I therefore command you not to rise on my
land and you are not to dare to wet the clothes or limbs of your master.'
The sea rose in the usual way and wetted the feet and legs of the monarch without showing any respect. The king accordingly leapt up and
said: 'Know all inhabitants of this earth, that vain and trivial is the
power of kings nor is anyone worthy of the name of king save Him
whose nod heaven and earth, and sea obey under laws eternal.' King
Cnut therefore, never again set the golden crown upon his neck, but set

it for ever above an image of the Lord which is nailed to a cross, in honour of God the great king. By his mercy may the soul of King Cnut rest in peace – from T. Forrester (ed.), *Henry of Huntingdon.*

From the *Knútsdrápa,* a Poem in Praise of King Cnut, by Ottar the Black

1. Destroyer of the chariot of the sea, you were of no great age when you pushed off your ships. Never, younger than you, did prince set out to take his part in war. Chief, you made ready your armoured ships, and were daring beyond measure. In your rage, Cnut, you mustered the red shields at sea.

2. The Jutes followed you out, they who were loath to flee. You arrayed the host of the men of Skane, free-handed adorner of Van's reindeer of the sail [a sailing ship. Van is Njörthr, a sea-god]. The wind filled the canvas, Prince, above your head. You turned all your prows westward out to sea. Where you went, you made your name renowned.

3. You carried the shield of war, and so dealt mightily, chief. I do not think, O Prince, that you cared much to sit at ease. Lord of the Jutes, you smote the race of Edgar in that raid. King's son, you dealt them a cruel blow. You are given the name of stubborn.

5. You made war in green Lindsey, Prince. The vikings wrought there what violence they would. In your rage, withstander of the Swedes, you brought sorrow upon the English, in *Helmingborg* to the west of the Ouse.

6. Young leader, you made the English fall close by the Tees. The deep dyke flowed over the bodies of Northumbrians. You broke the raven's sleep, waker of battle. Bold son of Swein, you led an attack at Sherstone, farther to the south.

7. . . . You shattered Brentford with its habitations. Edmund's noble offspring met with deadly wounds.

9. Gracious giver of mighty gifts you made corslets red in Norwich. You will lose your life before your courage fails.

10. Still you pressed on, blunting swords upon weapons; they could not defend their strongholds when you attacked. The bow screamed loud. You won no less renown, driver of the leaping steed of the roller, on Thames's bank. The wolf's jaw knew this well.

11. King bold in attack, you smote the Swedes in the place called Holy River, and there the she-wolf got much wolf's food. Terrible staff of

battle, you held the land against two princes [St Olaf and King Önund of Sweden], and the raven did not go hungry there. You are swift to deal with the race of men.

Translation by Margaret Ashdown,
English Historical Documents, Vol. I.

3. Silver penny of Archbishop Coelnoth of Canterbury struck by a moneyer Biarnwulf *c*. 860.

Hardacnut Becomes King of the English in 1040

Harold, king of the English, died at London, and was buried in Westminster. After his burial, the nobles of almost the whole of England sent envoys to Hardacnut at Bruges, where he was staying with his mother, and, thinking that they were acting advisably, asked him to come to England and take the sceptre of the kingdom. He prepared 60 ships, and manned them with Danish troops, sailed over to England before midsummer, and was received with rejoicing by all, and was soon raised to the throne of the kingdom; but during the time of his rule he did nothing worthy of royal power.

For, as soon as he began to reign, being not unmindful of the injuries which his predecessor King Harold, who was reputed his brother, had done either against him or against his mother, he sent to London Ælfric, archbishop of York, Earl Godwine, Stir, the master of his household, Eadric his steward, Thrond his executioner, and other men of high position, and ordered the body of this Harold to be dug up and thrown into a marsh; and when it had been thrown there, he gave orders for it to be pulled out and thrown into the River Thames. But a short time afterwards it was picked up by a certain fisherman and borne in haste to the Danes, and buried by them with honour in the cemetery which they had in London.

When this was done, he enjoined that eight marks were to be paid to each oarsman of his fleet, and twelve to each steersman, from the whole of England, a tribute so heavy, indeed, that hardly anyone could pay it; on which account he became extremely hateful to all who had before greatly desired his coming.

Besides these things, he burned with great anger against Earl Godwine and Lifing, bishop of Worcester, because of the killing of his brother Alfred, of which Ælfric, archbishop of York, and some others accused them. For that reason he deprived Lifing of the bishopric of Worcester and gave it to Ælfric; but the next year he took it from Ælfric and graciously gave it back to Lifing, who had made peace with him.

But Godwine gave to the king for his friendship a skilfully made galley, having a gilded prow, and furnished with the best tackle, handsomely equipped with suitable weapons and 80 picked soldiers, each of whom had on his arms two gold armlets, weighing 16 ounces, wore a triple mail-shirt, a partly gilded helmet on his head, and had a sword with a gilded hilt fastened round his loins, and a Danish battle-axe rimmed with gold and silver hanging from his left shoulder, and in his right hand a spear which in the English language is called *Ætgar* [a javelin]. Moreover, he swore to the king, with the ealdormen and the more important thegns of almost the whole of England, that it was not by his counsel nor his will that his brother was blinded, but that his lord King Harold had ordered him to do what he did — Florence of Worcester, *Chronicle of Chronicles*, edited by B. Thorpe.

King Edward the Confessor, 1042-1066

i. And not to omit his attitude and appearance, he was a very proper figure of a man — of outstanding height, and distinguished by his milky white hair and beard, full face and rosy cheeks, thin white hands, and long translucent fingers; in all the rest of his body he was an unblemished royal person. Pleasant, but always dignified, he walked with eyes downcast, most graciously affable to one and all. If some cause aroused his temper, he seemed as terrible as a lion, but he never revealed his anger by railing. To all petitioners he would either grant graciously or graciously deny, so that his gracious denial seemed the highest generosity. In public he carried himself as a true king and lord; in private with his courtiers as one of them, but with royal dignity unimpaired. He entrusted the cause of God to his bishops and to men skilled in canon law, warning them to act according to the case, and he ordered his secular judges, princes and palace lawyers to distinguish equitably, so that, on the one hand, righteousness should have royal support, and, on the other, evil, wherever it appeared, its just condemnation. This goodly king abrogated bad laws, with his witan established good ones, and filled with joy all that Britain over which by the grace of God and hereditary right he ruled.

ii. And so, with the kingdom made safe on all sides by those princes [Harold and Tostig], the most kindly King Edward passed life in security and peace, and spent much of his time in the glades and woods in the pleasures of hunting. After divine service, which he gladly and devoutly attended every day, he took much pleasure in hawks and birds of that kind which were brought before him, and was really delighted by the baying and scrambling of the hounds. In these and such like activities he sometimes spent the day, and it was in these alone that he seemed naturally inclined to snatch some worldly pleasure. Otherwise this man, of his free will devoted to God, lived in the squalor of the world like an angel, and 'at the accepted time' he zealously showed how assiduous he was in practising the Christian religion. What tongue or what page could unfold, in accordance with reality and true accounting, how kindly he received religious abbots and monks, above all foreign, whom he knew to be very devout and strict in their service to God, how humbly he joined in their conversation, and, at their departure, with what generosity he lavished himself on them? This he used to do throughout his reign; and since the news spread widely that such was his pleasure, he kept hospitality of this kind not only frequently but all

4. Silver coin with the portrait of King Alfred of Wessex, 871-901.

the time. Moreover, like a good father, he exhibited such men as models to the abbots and monks of his own kingdom, for monastic discipline had come to these more recently, and was on that account less strict. He used to stand with lamb-like meekness and tranquil mind at the holy offices of the divine mysteries and masses, a worshipper of Christ manifest to all the faithful; and at these times, unless he was addressed, he rarely spoke to anyone. Moreover, it was quietly, and only for the occasion — in any case, it should be distinctly said, with no mental pleasure — that he displayed the pomp of royal finery in which the queen obligingly arrayed him. And he would not have cared at all if it had been provided at far less cost. He was, however, grateful for the queen's solicitude in these matters, and with a certain kindness of feeling used to remark on her zeal most appreciatively to his intimates. He stooped with great mercy to the poor and infirm, and fully maintained many of these not only daily in his royal court but also at many places in his kingdom. Finally, his royal consort did not restrain him in those good works in which he prepared to lead the way, but rather urged speedier progress, and often enough seemed even to lead the way herself. For while he would give now and then, she was prodigal, but aimed her bounty to such good purpose as to consider the highest honour of the king as well. Although by custom and law a royal throne was always prepared for her at the king's side, she preferred, except in church and at the royal table, to sit at his feet, unless perchance he should reach out his hand to her, or with a gesture of the hand invite or command her to sit next to him. She was, I say, a woman to be placed before all noble matrons or persons of royal and imperial rank as a model of virtue and integrity for maintaining both the practices of Christian religion and worldly dignity. Although in the earthly kingdom great prosperity smiled upon them, occasionally, however, in the plots of certain insurgents adversity struck with force. But not such as could cripple a realm ruled by so great a king; indeed, the kingdom, employing the brother earls mentioned before as its protectors, most quickly either assuaged it or with military valour stamped it out — from Frank Barlow (ed.), *The Life of King Edward The Confessor.*

2 Towns and Buildings

The Bishop Saves Part of Canterbury From Destruction By Fire, 619

... it happened once that the city of Canterbury, being by carelessness set on fire, was in danger of being consumed by the spreading conflagration; water was thrown over the fire in vain; a considerable part of the city was already destroyed, and the fierce flame advancing towards the bishop, when he, confiding in the Divine assistance, where human failed, ordered himself to be carried towards the raging fire, that was spreading on every side. The church of the Four Crowned Martyrs was in the place where the fire raged most. The bishop being carried thither by his servants, the sick man averted the danger by prayer, which a number of strong men had not been able to perform by much labour. Immediately, the wind, which blowing from the south had spread the conflagration throughout the city, turning to the north, prevented the destruction of those places that had lain in its way, and then ceasing entirely, the flames were abundantly extinguished. And thus the man of God, whose mind was inflamed with the fire of Divine charity, and who was wont to drive away the powers of the air by his frequent prayers, from doing harm to himself, or his people, was deservedly allowed to prevail over the worldly winds and flames, and to obtain that they should not injure him or his — Bede, *Ecclesiastical History*, translated by J.A. Giles.

Fire! The House Burnt Down But Not That Wooden Post, *c.* 645

... Another person of the British nation, as is reported, happened to travel by the same place, where the aforesaid battle [of Maserfield] was fought, and observing one particular spot of ground greener and more beautiful than any other part of the field he judiciously concluded with

5. These fields at Braunton, Devon, show the strip system of early farming.

himself that there could be no other cause for that unusual greenness, but that some person of more holiness than any other in the army had been killed there. He therefore took along with him some of the earth, tying it up in a linen cloth, supposing it would some time or other be of use for curing sick people, and proceeding on his journey, came at night to a certain village, and entered a house where the neighbours were feasting at supper; and received by the owners of the house, he sat down with them at the entertainment, hanging the cloth, in which he had brought the earth, on a post against the wall. They sat long at supper and drank hard, with a great fire in the middle of the room; it happened that the sparks flew up and caught the top of the house, which being made of wattles and thatch, was presently in a flame; the guests ran out in a fright, without being able to put a stop to the fire. The house was consequently burnt down, only that post on which the earth hung remained entire and untouched. On observing this, they were all amazed, and inquiring into it diligently, understood that the earth had been taken from the place where the blood of King Oswald had been shed. . . . – Bede, *Ecclesiastical History*, translated by J.A. Giles.

6. A reconstruction of one of the royal manors of the kings of Wessex, at Cheddar in Somerset. Dr P.A. Rahtz, who directed the excavation, 'isolated ninth-, tenth- and eleventh-century features, revealing the development of the residence over many years'.

Cogitosus, The Biographer of Saint Brigit, Describes the Great Church of Kildare as it Was. *c.* 650

I must not omit the miracle which attended the repairs to the church in which rest the bodies of Bishop Conlaed and the virgin Saint Brigit. They are placed in elaborate monuments, to right and left of the decorated altar, and are splendidly bedecked with gold and silver, jewels and precious stones, and have gold and silver crowns hanging above them.

As the numbers of the faithful of both sexes grew, the church was extended, both in area at ground level and in height projecting upwards, and was decorated with paintings. It has three oratories within, divided by painted walls, under a single roof that spans the larger building.

In the eastern part, a cross wall extends from one wall to the opposite wall, decorated with pictures and covered with linen. In its ends are two doors. Through the southern door the Bishop enters with his regular choir and those deputed to celebrate the rites and sacrifices to the Lord. Through the other door, in the northern part of the cross wall, the Abbess enters with her girls and faithful widows to enjoy the feast of the body and blood of Jesus Christ. Another wall extends from the eastern part as far as the cross wall, and divides the paved floor of the buildings into two equal parts.

The church has many windows, and on the south side one ornamented gate, through which the priests and the faithful people of the male sex enter the church, and another gate on the north side, through which the congregation of virgins and faithful women enter. So in one great basilica a large number of people may pray with one heart to Almighty God, in different places according to their orders and ranks and sexes, with walls between them.

When the workmen set on its hinges the old door of the north gate, through which Saint Brigit used to enter the church, it could not cover all the newly constructed gate . . . unless a quarter were added to the door's height. When the workmen were deliberating whether to make a new and larger door, or whether to make a picture and add it to the old door . . . the leading craftsman of all Ireland gave wise advice, to pray that night to the Lord, with Saint Brigit. Next morning the old door covered the whole gateway — Cogitosus, *Vita Brigit, 35.*

A Year of Ice and Fire, 764

An immense snowfall, hardened into ice, unparalleled in all former ages, oppressed the land from the beginning of winter almost until the middle of spring; through its severity the trees and plants for the most part withered, and many marine animals were found dead . . .

In the same year many towns, monasteries and villages in various districts and kingdoms were suddenly devastated by fire; for instance, the calamity struck Stretburg, Winchester, Southampton, the city of London, the city of York, Doncaster and many other places . . .

— Simeon of Durham, *Historia Regum, English Historical Documents*, Vol. I.

7. Aerial view of Tintagel Castle, Cornwall, looking to the south. The white escarpment on the right shows where parts of the upper and lower wards have fallen into the sea. Tintagel is associated with the birth of Arthur, and the famous legend goes back to the fifth or sixth century.

A Tenth-Century Land Grant, 926

Therefore I, Athelstan, king of the Anglo-Saxons, adorned and elevated with no small dignity, prompted by desire from on high, will grant to my faithful thegn Ealdred the land of five hides which is called Chalgrave and Tebworth, which he bought with sufficient money of his own, namely ten pounds of gold and silver, from the pagans by the order of King Edward and also of Ealdorman Ethelred along with the other ealdormen and thegns; conceding with it the freedom of hereditary right, to have and possess as long as he lives, and to give after his death to whatever heirs, acceptable to himself, he shall wish.

These are the boundaries of the aforesaid land: Where the dyke runs into Watling Street, along Watling Street to the ford, then along the brook to the other ford, then from that ford up to the spring, and thence into the valley, thence from the valley to the dyke, from the dyke to the second dyke, then from that dyke to the brook, then from the brook to Kimberwell, then along the dyke to Eastcote, then thence to the old brook, up from the old brook parallel with the little stream, then straight up to the highway, along the highway to the dyke, along the dyke to Watling Street.

And the donation of the aforesaid land is to be free from every secular burden except military service and the construction of bridges and fortresses, in return for an adequate sum of money which I have received from him, i.e. 150 mancuses of pure gold – tenth-century Charter, *English Historical Documents*, Vol. I.

The Ruin

This elegy on a ruined city with its fallen walls and departed glory is taken by many to refer to the city of Bath.

Wondrous is this wall-stone; broken by fate, the castles have decayed; the work of giants is crumbling. Roofs are fallen, ruinous are the towers, despoiled are the towers with their gates; frost is on their cement, broken are the roofs, cut away, fallen, undermined by age. The grasp of the earth, stout grip of the ground, holds its mighty builders, who have perished and gone; till now a hundred generations of men have died. Often this wall, grey with lichen and stained with red, unmoved under storms, has survived kingdom after kingdom; its lofty gate has fallen . . . the bold in spirit bound the foundation of the wall wondrously together with wires. Bright were the castle-dwellings, many the bath-houses, lofty the host of pinnacles, great the tumult of men, many a mead hall full of the joys of men, till Fate the mighty overturned that. The wide walls fell; days of pestilence came; death swept away all the bravery of men; their fortresses became waste places; the city fell to ruin. The multitudes who might have built it anew lay dead on the earth. Wherefore these courts are in decay and these lofty gates; the woodwork of the roof is stripped of tiles; the place has sunk into ruin, levelled to the hills, where in times past many a man light of heart and

8. Saxon tower, All Saints Church, Earls Barton, Northamptonshire, the finest example of Anglo-Saxon architecture. The 'long and short work' at the quoins, and the 'pilaster-strip', narrow bands of projecting stonework, are characteristic.

bright with gold, adorned with splendours, proud and flushed with wine, shone in war trappings, gazed on treasure, on silver, on precious stones, on riches, on possessions, on costly gems, on this bright castle of the broad kingdom. Stone courts stood here; the stream with its great gush sprang forth hotly; the wall enclosed all within its bright bosom; there the baths were hot in its centre; that was spacious . . . – *Anglo-Saxon Poetry*, translated by R.K. Gordon.

Survey of an Estate at Tidenham, Gloucestershire, *c.* 1060

In Tidenham there are 30 hides made up of 9 hides of demesne-land and 21 hides of land occupied [by the tenants]. At Stroat there are 12 hides, including 27 yardlands of rent-paying land and 30 basket weirs on the Severn. At Milton 5 hides, including 14 yardlands of rent-paying land, 14 basket weirs on the Severn and 2 hackle weirs on the Wye. At 'Kingston' there are 5 hides, including 13 yardlands of rent-paying land, and 1 hide above the dyke is now rent-paying land also, and what is there outside the enclosed land is still partly in demesne, partly let for rent to the Welsh sailors. At 'Kingston' there are 21 basket weirs on the Severn and 12 on the Wye. At Bishton there are 3 hides and 15 basket weirs on the Wye. In Landcaut there are 3 hides and 2 hackle weirs on the Wye and 9 basket weirs. Throughout the whole estate 12 pence is due from every yardland and 4 pence as alms. At every weir within the 30 hides every alternate fish belongs to the lord of the manor, and every rare fish which is of value – sturgeon or porpoise, herring or sea fish – and no one has the right of selling any fish for money when the lord is on the estate without informing him about it. From Tidenham much labour is due. The *geneat* must labour either on the estate or off the estate, whichever he is bidden, and ride and furnish carrying service and supply transport and drive herds and do many other things. The boor must do what is due from him – he must plough half an acre as week-work and himself fetch the seed from the lord's barn, and a whole acre for church dues from his own barn. For weir building he must supply 40 larger rods or a fother of small rods, or he shall build 8 yokes for 3 ebb tides, supply 15 poles of field fencing or dig 5, fence and dig 1 pole of the manor-house hedge, reap 1½ acres, and mow half an acre, and work at other kinds of work, always in proportion to the work. He shall give 6 pence after Easter and half a sester of honey, at Lammas 6 sesters of malt, at Martinmas a ball of good net yarn. On the same estate it is the rule that he who has 7 swine shall give 3 and thereafter always the tenth, and in spite of this pay for the right of having mast when there is mast — *Anglo-Saxon Charters.*

9. Early English head-dresses, from *Douce Apocalyse.*

3 Family

Rights and Dignities to Men Who Prosper

1. Once it used to be that people and rights went by dignities, and councillors of the people were then entitled to honour, each according to his rank, whether noble or ceorl, retainer or lord.

2. And if a ceorl prospered, that he possessed fully five hides of land of his own, a bell and a castle-gate, a seat and a special office in the king's hall, then he was henceforth entitled to the rights of a thegn.

3. And the thegn who prospered, that he served the king and rode in his household band on his missions, if he himself had a thegn who served him, possessing five hides on which he discharged the king's dues, and who attended his lord in the king's hall, and had thrice gone on his errand to the king — then he was afterwards allowed to represent his lord with his preliminary oath, and legally obtain his right to pursue a charge, wherever he needed.

4. And he who had no such distinguished representative, swore in person to obtain his rights, or lost his case.

5. And if a thegn prospered, that he became an earl, then he was afterwards entitled to an earl's rights.

6. And if a trader prospered, that he crossed thrice the open sea at his own expense, then he was afterwards entitled to the rights of a thegn — Concerning Wergilds and Dignities, *English Historical Documents*, Vol. I.

Religious Husband and Wife

Holy books teach what every faithful man should do when first he leads his lawful wife home; that is, according to the teaching of the books, to keep their chastity for the space of three days and three nights and on the third day to be present at Mass and both to take the Eucharist and then to keep his marriage before God and the world as is needful for them. And all wives should keep their chastity for 49 days and nights before Easter and all through Easter week, and always on the night of the Lord's day, and Wednesday and Friday. And every religious woman should keep her chastity for 3 months before childbirth and for 60 nights and days after, whether the child be male or female — Penitential of Archbishop Ecgbert (735-66), B. Thorpe, *Ancient Laws and Institutes of England.*

10. A thegn, one who held land of the king or other superior by military service.

Betrothing a Woman, *c.* 940

1. If a man desire to betroth a maiden or a woman, and it so be agreeable to her and her friends, then is it right that the bridegroom, according to the law of God, and according to the customs of the world, first promise, and give a 'wed' [pledge] to those who are her 'foresprecas', that he desire her, in such wise that he will keep her, according to God's law, as a husband shall his wife: and let his friends guarantee that.

2. After that, it is to be known to whom the 'foster-lean' [expense of having a child reared] belongs: let the bridegroom give a 'wed' [pledge] for this; and let his friends guarantee it.

3. Then, after that, let the bridegroom declare what he will grant her,

in case she choose his will [accept him as her lord], and what he will grant her, if she live longer than he.

4. If it be so agreed, then is it right that she be entitled to half the property, and to all, if they have children in common, except she again choose a husband.

5. Let him confirm all that which he has promised with a 'wed' [pledge]; and let his friends guarantee that.

6. If they then are agreed in every thing, then let the kinsmen take it in hand, and betroth their kinswoman to wife, and to a righteous life, to him who desired her, and let him take possession of the 'born' [surety] who has control of the 'wed' [pledge].

7. But if a man desire to lead her out of the land, into another thane's land, then it will be advisable for her that her friends have an agreement that no wrong shall be done to her; and if she commit a fault, that they may be nearest in the 'bot' [compensation], if she have not whereof she can make 'the bot'.

8. At the nuptials, there shall be a mass-priest by law; who shall with God's blessing bind their union to all prosperity.

9. Well is it also to be looked to, that it be known, that they, through kinship, be not too nearly allied; lest that be afterwards divided, which before was wrongly joined — Laws of King Edmund, 940-6, B. Thorpe, *Ancient Laws and Institutes of England.*

Leather Pouches, 975

I saw a creature. Behind it was its belly,
hugely distended. It was served by an attendant.
a man of great strength . . .
It never dies when it must give
What is inside it to the other, but this is restored again
in its bosom, its breath is revived.
It creates a son and is its own father.

Old English Riddle in *The Exeter Book*, pt ii,
translated by W.S. Mackie, Early English Text Society.

11. Curtained beds in Saxon England.

Widows, Tenth Century

It is right that widows earnestly follow the example of Anna, who was in the temple day and night, zealously serving; she fasted very often, and was devoted to prayers, and with groaning mind called to Christ, and distributed alms, oft and frequently, and ever propitiated God, as much as she was able, by word and deed, and has now for reward heavenly mirth. So should a good widow obey her lord — Saxon Institutes of Polity, Civil and Ecclesiastical, B. Thorpe, *Ancient Laws and Institutes of England.*

4 Food and Drink

How Bishop Wilfred Saved Sussex from Further Famine, 681

But Bishop Wilfrid, by preaching to them, not only delivered them from the misery of perpetual damnation, but also from an inexpressible calamity of temporal death, for no rain had fallen in that province in three years before his arrival, whereupon a dreadful famine ensued, which cruelly destroyed the people. In short, it is reported, that very often forty or fifty men, being spent with want, would go together to some precipice, or to the sea-shore, and there, hand in hand, perish by the fall, or be swallowed up by the waves. But on the very day on which the nation received the baptism of faith, there fell a soft but plentiful rain . . . [Wilfrid] , when he came into the province, and found so great misery from famine, taught them to get food by fishing; for their sea and rivers abounded in fish, but the people had no skill to take them, except eels alone. The bishop's men having gathered eel nets everywhere, cast them into the sea, and by the blessing of God took three hundred fishes of several sorts. . . . – Bede, *Ecclesiastical History of England*, account of St Wilfrid and the famine, translated by J.A. Giles.

Avoid Meat of Animals Killed by Wolves, *c.* 740

If a wolf rend any manner of cattle and thereafter it die, let no Christian taste thereof. If any man do this let him fast on bread and water for 4 weeks. If the beast live and afterwards be slain, then it can be freely eaten – Penitential of Archbishop Ecgbert, 735-66, B. Thorpe, *Ancient Laws and Institutes of England.*

Clean and Unclean Food Explained, *c.* 750

You may eat fish although it has been found dead because it is not of our nature. Horse flesh is allowed, although many people will not eat it. Birds and other creatures found strangled in nets are not to be eaten; even if a hawk pecked them if they are found dead they are not to be eaten for in the Acts of the Apostles it is commanded to keep yourselves from fornication and from things strangled and from blood and from idolatry. You may eat a hare and it is good against dysentery and diarrhoea if sodden in water. And mixed with pepper its liver is good for mouth-ache.

If bees kill a man let them be killed at once before they reach the honey, at any rate so that they do not stay there through the night; and let the honey which they have made be eaten. If a young pig fall into liquor and is taken out alive, let the liquor be sprinkled with holy water and fumigated with incense and let the liquor be taken; if it is dead and the liquor cannot be given let it be poured out. If any one touch any food with impure hands, or if a dog, or a cat, or a mouse touch it or any unclean animal, [Archbishop] Theodore has said that it comes to no harm. But if a mouse or a weasel fall into much liquor and die there let it be sprinkled with holy water and taken. No harm comes if any from necessity eat an unclean animal. A sick man may take food at any hour whatsoever and whenever he wish. . . .

If pigs eat any dead flesh or taste any human blood we do not think that they need be cast out; but it is not lawful to eat them until they are clean. If a hen drink human blood, it is lawful to eat it after 3 months; but on this point we have not ancient authority. If anyone eat anything with blood in half cooked food, if consciously, he is to fast 7 days, if unconsciously, for 3 days or to sing the Psalter. If anyone unconsciously drinks his own blood in his saliva, there is no peril. If anyone eat anything from that of which a dog or a mouse has eaten or which a weasel had defiled, if consciously, he is to sing 100 psalms, if unconsciously, 50 psalms. If anyone gives to another liquor in which a mouse or a weasel has been drowned, if he is a layman, let him fast 3 days; if he is a monk, let him sing 100 psalms. If he knew it not at first but knew it later, let him sing the Psalter — Confessional of Archbishop Ecgbert (735-66), *Ancient Laws and Institutes of England.*

Mead, the Honey Drink, 975

I am of value to men, found far and wide,
brought from the woods and the fortress-like hills,
from the valleys and the downs. In the day-time wings
carried me in the air, and bore me skilfully
under the shelter of a roof. Afterwards men
washed me in a tub. Now I am a binder
and a scourger, and soon become a thrower;
sometimes I cast an old fellow right to the ground.
Soon he discovers, he who grapples with me
and fights against my mighty assault,
that he must hit the ground with his back,
if he has not already desisted from his folly.
Robbed of his strength, loud in speech,
deprived of his might, he has no control over his mind,
his feet, or his hands. . . . Discover what I am called
who thus bind men upon earth
till they are dazed by my blows in the light of day.

> Old English Riddle in *The Exeter Book*,
> Early English Text Society, O.S.

12. Anglo-Saxon banquet — the toast.

5 Education

Irish Learning Was Imitated in the Sixth Century, Monasteries Multiplied, Books Copied

The old learning of Rome had gone. New education had come, but not to all countries.

Culture and education are dying out, perishing throughout the cities of Gaul . . . There is no grammarian to be found, skilful enough in dialectic to depict the present age in prose or verse. You often hear people complaining 'Alas for our times; literacy is dying among us, and no man can be found among our peoples who is capable of setting down the deeds of the present on paper' – Gregory of Tours, *History of the Franks*. From John Morris, *The Age of Arthur*.

Monastic Studies

Rule of St Benedict of Nursia about 520 for the monastery he founded at Monte Cassino between Rome and Naples. This had some effect upon the Celtic Church.

Of Daily Handiwork. Idleness is the enemy of the soul; therefore the brethren should be occupied at certain times in working with their hands, and at certain other hours in godly reading.

Wherefore we think fit thus to dispose both these times. From Easter to the first of October let them go forth early and labour at necessary work from Prime [six a.m.] until almost the fourth hour; and from the fourth until about the sixth let them busy themselves with reading . . . From the first of October until the beginning of Lent, let them read a full hour until the second hour; then let them say Tierce [office of third hour], and let all work until None [the third quarter of the day] at the work enjoined them . . . After reflection let them busy themselves with their reading, or with the Psalms.

Again, in Lententide, let them read from early morn to full tenth hour with whatsoever work has been enjoined upon them. And in these days of Lent let each take one volume for himself from the library, and let him read that book fully from beginning to end [during that year]. These volumes must be given out on the first day of Lent.

13. The Sutton Hoo ship, *c.* 655. The grave at Sutton Hoo near Woodbridge, Suffolk 'produced the richest and most brilliant treasure ever found on British soil; it is indeed only paralleled in Europe by the funerary treasure of Childeric, King of the Franks who died in 481. . . The ship was a rowing-boat, about eighty-six feet long . . . The treasures found in the grave leave no doubt that this was the memorial of a king', D.M. Wilson.

But, above all, let one or two seniors be deputed to go round the monastery at those hours which are assigned for reading, lest perchance some slothful brother be found who spends his time in idleness or in talk, and who is not intent upon his reading, thus wasting not only his own time but that of others also. If such a one be found (though God forbid there should be such!) let him be admonished once and twice; and, if he amend not then, let him be subjected to regular discipline [to corporal punishment], that the rest may fear to follow his steps.

On Sundays let them spend their time in reading, except those who are deputed for the various services. But if any monk be so negligent and idle that he will not or cannot meditate or read, let some work be enjoined upon him, that he be not wholly unoccupied — from G.G.

Coulton, *Social Life in Britain from the Conquest to the Reformation.*

Ease of Irish Educational System in the Seventh Century

There were many Englishmen in Ireland, both noble and plebeian, who left their homeland in the time of bishops Finan and Colman either to read Divinity or to live more continently. Some soon bound themselves to a monastic vow, but others preferred to travel around the cells of different teachers for the joy of reading. The Irish welcomed them all, gave them food and lodging without charge, lent them their books to read and taught them without fee — Bede, *Historia Ecclesiastica Gentis Anglorum*, edited by C. Plummer.

Alcuin of York Describes Education in a Monastic School in the Eighth Century

The learned Albert gave drink to thirsty minds at the fountain of the sciences. To some he communicated the art and the rules of grammar; for others he caused floods of rhetoric to flow; he knew how to exercise these in the battles of jurisprudence, and those in the songs of Adonia; some learned from him to pipe Castilian airs and with lyric foot to strike the summit of Parnassus; to others he made known the harmony of the heavens, the courses of the sun and the moon, the five zones of the pole, the seven planets, the laws of the course of the stars, the motions of the sea, earthquakes, the nature of men, and of beasts, and of birds, and of all that inhabit the forest. He unfolded the different qualities and combinations of numbers; he taught how to calculate with certainty the solemn return of Eastertide, and above all, he explained the mysteries of the Holy Scriptures — *Alcuin of York*, translated by G.F. Browne.

Mastering Arithmetic, *c.* 700

As to the principles of arithmetic what shall be said? when the despair of doing sums oppressed my mind so that all the previous labours spent on learning, whose most secret chamber I thought I knew already, seemed nothing, and to use Jerome's expression I who before thought myself a past master began again to be a pupil, until the difficulty solved itself, and at last, by God's grace, I grasped after incessant study the most difficult of all things, what they call fractions – letter to Bishop Haeddi by Aldhelm (d. 709), translated by A.F. Leach, *Educational Charters and Documents, 598 to 1909.*

14. The flap of a purse, decorated with gold, glass and garnets. From the ship-burial, Sutton Hoo, Suffolk, seventh century.

Childhood and Upbringing of Alfred the Great, 864

Chap. 22: Now he was loved by his father and mother, and indeed by everybody with a united and immense love, more than all his brothers, and was always brought up in the royal court, and as he passed through all his childhood and boyhood he appeared fairer in form than all his brothers, and more pleasing in his looks, his words and his ways. And from his cradle a longing for wisdom before all things and among all the pursuits of this present life, combined with his noble birth, filled the noble temper of his mind; but alas, by the unworthy carelessness of his parents and tutors, he remained ignorant of letters until his twelfth year or even longer. But he listened attentively to Saxon poems day and night, and hearing them often recited by others committed them to his retentive memory. A keen huntsman, he toiled unceasingly in every branch of hunting, and not in vain; for he was without equal in his skill and good fortune in that art, as also in all other gifts of God, as we have ourselves often seen.

Chap. 23: When, therefore, his mother one day was showing him and his brothers a certain book of Saxon poetry which she held in her hand, she said; 'I will give this book to whichever of you can learn it most quickly,' And moved by these words, or rather by divine inspiration, and attracted by the beauty of the initial letter of the book, Alfred said in reply to his mother, forestalling his brothers, his elders in years though not in grace: 'Will you really give this book to one of us, to the one who can soonest understand and repeat it to you?' And, smiling and rejoicing, she confirmed it, saying: 'To him will I give it.' Then taking the book from her hand he immediately went to his master, who read it. And when it was read, he went back to his mother and repeated it.

Chap. 24: After this he learnt the daily course, that is the services of the hours, and then certain psalms and many prayers. He collected these into one book and carried it about with him everywhere in his bosom (as I have myself seen) day and night, for the sake of prayer, through all the changes of this present life, and was never parted from it. But alas, what he principally desired, the liberal arts, he did not obtain according to his wish, because, as he was wont to say, there were at that time no good scholars in all the kingdom of the West Saxons.

Chap. 25: He often affirmed with frequent laments and sighs from the bottom of his heart, that among all his difficulties and hindrances in this present life this was the greatest: that, during the time when he had youth and leisure and aptitude for learning, he had no teachers; but when he was more advanced in years, he did have teachers and writers to some extent, when he was not able to study, because he was harassed, nay, rather disturbed, day and night both with illnesses unknown to all the physicians of this island, and with the cares of the royal office at home and abroad, and also with the invasions of pagans by land and sea. Yet, among all the difficulties of this present life, from infancy until the present-day, he has never abandoned that same insatiable longing, and even now yearns for it — *Asser, Life of King Alfred*, translated by L.C. Jane.

King Alfred Shows his Love of Learning, 884

Ethelwerd, the youngest of Alfred's children, by the divine counsels and the admirable prudence of the king, was consigned to the schools

15. Part of a late eighth-
century manuscript of
Bede's *Historia
Ecclesiastica Gentis
Anglorum.*

In the above-mentioned year, when there was an eclipse, swiftly followed by a plague, during which Colman was defeated by the unani-
mous arguments of the Catholics and returned to his own folk,
Deusdedit the sixth Bishop of the church in Canterbury died on the day
before the Ides of July [14 July]. But Erconberct King of Kent, dying
in the same month and on the same day, left his royal seat to his son
Ecgberct — translation of the passage by Henry Marsh.

of learning, where, with the children of almost all the nobility of the country, and many also who were not noble, he prospered under the diligent care of his teachers. Books in both languages, namely, Latin and Saxon, were read in the school. They also learned to write; so that before they were of an age to practise many arts, namely, hunting and such pursuits as befit noblemen, they became studious and clever in the liberal arts . . .

In the meantime the king, during the frequent wars and other trammels of this present life, the invasion of the pagans, and his own daily infirmities of body, continued to carry on the government and to exercise hunting in all its branches; to teach his workers in gold and artificers of all kinds, his falconers, hawkers, and dogkeepers; to build houses, majestic and good, beyond all the precedents of his ancestors, by his new mechanical inventions; to recite the Saxon books, and especially to learn by heart the Saxon poems, and to make others learn them.

He alone never desisted from studying most diligently to the best of his ability. He attended mass and other daily services of religion. He was frequent in psalm-singing and prayer at the hours both of the day and night. He also went to the churches in the night-time to pray, secretly and unknown to his courtiers. He bestowed alms and largesses on both natives and foreigners of all countries. He was affable and pleasant to all, and curiously eager to investigate things unknown. Many Franks, Frisians, Gauls, pagans, Britons, Scots, and Armoricans, noble and ignoble, submitted voluntarily to his dominion.

But God at that time, as some consolation to the king's benevolence, yielding to his complaint, sent certain lights to illuminate him, namely, Werefrith, bishop of the church of Worcester, a man well versed in Divine Scripture, who, by the king's command, first turned the book of the Dialogues of Pope Gregory and Peter, his disciple, from Latin into Saxon, and sometimes putting sense for sense interpreted them with clearness and elegance. After him was Plegmund, a Mercian by birth, archbishop of the church of Canterbury, a venerable man and endowed with wisdom; Ethelstan, also, and Werewulf, his priests and chaplains, Mercians by birth and learned men. These four had been invited out of Mercia by King Alfred, who exalted them with many honours in the Kingdom of the West Saxons. By their teaching and wisdom the king's desires increased increasingly, and were gratified. Night and day, whenever he had leisure, he commanded such men as these to read books to him — for he never suffered himself to be without one of them — and thus he acquired a knowledge of every book.

But the king's commendable avarice could not be gratified even by this, for he sent messengers beyond the sea to Gaul to procure teachers, and he invited from thence Grimbald, priest and monk, a venerable man and good singer, adorned with every kind of ecclesiastical discipline and good morals, and most learned in Holy Scripture. He also obtained from thence John, also priest and monk, a man of most energetic talents and learned in all kinds of literary science, and skilled in many other arts. By the teaching of these two men the king's mind was much enlarged, and he enriched and honoured them with much influence — Asser, *Life of King Alfred*, translated by J.A. Giles in *Six English Chronicles*.

King Alfred on Improving Education, 894

King Alfred's preface to his translation into English of Pope Gregory's Cura Pastoralis. *Alfred refers to the decline in learning in Wessex and his intention to restore it.*

King Alfred bids greet bishop Waerferth with his words in loving and friendly wise: and I would have thee know that it has come very often into my mind, what wise counsellors there were of old throughout England, both spiritual and lay; and how happy were those times then throughout England; and how the kings who had the authority over the folk obeyed God and his messengers; and they both maintained peace, and morals, and authority within their kingdom, and also extended their borders; and what good success they had both with warfare and with wisdom; and also the spiritual orders, how eager they were both in teaching and in learning, and in all the services they owed to God; and how strangers came hither to this land in search of wisdom and learning; and how we now must get these things from abroad, if we are to have them. So utterly was learning fallen off in England that there were very few on this side of the Humber who could understand their service-books in English, or translate even a letter from Latin into English: and I ween that there were not many beyond the Humber. So few were there of them that I cannot remember even a single one south of the Thames when I succeeded to the Kingdom. Thanks be to Almighty God that we have now any supply of teachers. And so, I bid thee to do as I believe that thou thyself dost wish, that thou rid thyself of the cares of this world, as often as thou canst, that thou mayest apply the wisdom which God has given thee, wherever thou canst. Bethink thee what temporal punishments came upon us, in that we neither loved wisdom ourselves nor suffered other men to have it; we loved the name of Christian only, and very few of us loved the Christian virtues.

When I called all this to mind, then I remember also how I had seen, before it was all harried and burnt up, how the churches throughout all England stood filled with treasures and books. And there was also a great multitude of God's servants, but they could make very little use of the books, because they were not written in their own speech. As if they had said: 'Our forefathers, who held these places before us, loved wisdom, and through wisdom they got wealth, and left it to us. Here their track may still be seen, but we cannot follow it up, and so we have lost both the wealth and the wisdom, because we would not bend our minds to following the track.'

Then, when I remembered all this, I wondered greatly concerning men of wise and good counsel who of old were throughout England, and had learned all these books fully, that they would turn no part of them into their own tongue. But then I soon made answer to myself and said: 'They did not ween that ever men would become so reckless, and learning so fall away; it was from deliberate purpose that they abstained from doing it, and wished that there should be greater wisdom here in this land, as we knew more tongues. . . .'

Therefore it seems better to me, if it seems also to you that we too should turn into the tongue which we can all understand certain books which are most necessary for all men to know; and that we bring it about (as we very easily may, with God's help, if we have peace) that all the youth which now is in England of freemen who have wealth enough to be able to apply themselves to it, be set to learning, so long as they are good for no other business, till the time that they can well read anything written in English; let those, who are to be taught further, and set apart for a higher office be taught further in Latin.

When I remembered how the knowledge of Latin had before this fallen away throughout England, and yet many could read what was written in English, then I began, among the other diverse and manifold cares of this kingdom, to turn into English the book which is called in Latin *Pastoralis* and in English *Shepherd's Book*, sometimes word by word, sometimes sense by sense, as I learnt it from Plegmund my archbishop, and from Asser my bishop, and from Grimbald my mass-priest and from John my mass-priest. And when I had learnt it, as best I could understand it, as I could most clearly interpret it, I turned it into English; and to every bishopric in my kingdom will I send one. . . —
King Alfred, translated by R.W. Chambers, *England Before the Norman Conquest.*

Education of the Children of a King, 912

Edward [the son of Alfred] brought up his daughters in such wise, that in childhood they gave their whole attention to literature, and afterwards employed themselves in the labours of the distaff and needle . . . His sons were so educated, as, first, to have the completest benefit of learning, that afterwards they might succeed to govern the State, not like rustics, but philosophers — William of Malmesbury, *Chronicle*, II, v, translated by J.A. Giles.

Of Schools, Tenth Century

xix. Of schools in churches.
      If any priest wish to send his nephew or other kinsman to be taught in the churches which are entrusted to our governance, we willingly grant him this.
xx.   That priests shall keep schools in the villages and teach small boys freely.
      Priests ought always to have schools of schoolmasters in their houses, and if any of the faithful wish to give his little ones to learning they ought willingly to receive them and teach them for nothing. You should think that it has been written (Daniel xii. 3) 'The learned shall shine as the brightness of the firmament' and that 'those who have educated and taught many to righteousness shall shine as the stars for ever'. But they ought not to expect anything from their relations except what they wish to do of their own accord — Council of 994 Book of Ecclesiastical Laws, A.F. Leach, *Educational Charters and Documents, 598 to 1909.*

King Alfred Obtains Teachers from Abroad. Asser Came in from Wales. Tenth Century

He [Alfred] sent messengers beyond the sea to Gaul, to procure teachers, and he invited from thence Grimbald, priest and monk, a venerable man, and good singer, adorned with every kind of ecclesiastical discipline and good morals, and most learned in holy scripture. He also

obtained from thence John, also priest and monk, a man of most energetic talents, and learned in all kinds of literary science, and skilled in
many other arts. By the teaching of these men the king's mind was
much enlarged, and he enriched and honoured them with much influence.

In these times, I also came into Saxony [Wessex] out of the furthest
coasts of Western Britain; and when I had proposed to go to him
through many intervening provinces, I arrived in the country of the
Saxons, who live on the right hand, which in Saxon is called Sussex,
under the guidance of some of that nation; and there I first saw him in
the royal vill, which is called Dene. He received me with kindness, and
among other familiar conversation, he asked me eagerly to devote
myself to his service and become his friend, to leave everything which I
possessed on the left, or western bank of the Severn, and he promised
he would give more than an equivalent for it in his own dominions. I
replied that I could not incautiously and rashly promise such things; for
it seemed to me unjust, that I should leave those sacred places in which
I had been bred, educated, and crowned, and at last ordained, for the
sake of any earthly honour and power, unless by compulsion. Upon this,
he said, 'if you cannot accede to this, at least, let me have your service
in part: spend six months of the year with me here, and the other six in
Britain'. To this, I replied, 'I could not even promise that easily or hastily
without the advice of my friends'. At length, however, when I perceived
that he was anxious for my services, though I knew not why, I promised him that, if my life was spared, I would return to him after six
months, with such a reply as should be agreeable to him as well as
advantageous to me and mine. With this answer he was satisfied, and
when I had given him a pledge to return at the appointed time, on the
fourth day we left him and returned on horseback towards our own
country.

After our departure, a violent fever seized me in the city of Winchester, where I lay for twelve months and one week, night and day, without
hope of recovery. At the appointed time, therefore, I could not fulfil
my promise of visiting him, and he sent messengers to hasten my journey, and to inquire the cause of my delay. As I was unable to ride to
him, I sent a second messenger to tell him the cause of my delay, and
assure him that, if I recovered from my infirmity, I would fulfil what I
had promised. My complaint left me, and by the advice and consent of
all my friends, for the benefit of that holy place, and of all who dwelt
therein [St. Davids] I did as I had promised to the king, and devoted
myself to his service, on the condition that I should remain with him

six months in every year, either continuously, if I could spend six months with him at once, or alternately, three months in Britain [Wales] and three in Saxony [Wessex]. For my friends hoped that they should sustain less tribulation and harm from King Hemeid, who often plundered that monastery and the parish of St. Deguus, and sometimes expelled the prelates, as they expelled archbishop Novis, my relation, and myself; if in any manner I could secure the notice and friendship of the king — Asser, *Life of King Alfred*, translated by J.A. Giles in *Six English Chronicles*.

Aelfric's English Pupils, 1005

Aelfric was Abbot of Evesham and his teaching method of question and answer was used for several hundred years.

Pupil. We boys beseech thee, O master, teach us to speak Latin rightly; for we are unlearned, and speak corruptly.

Master. What will ye speak?

Pupil. What care we, so that we only speak rightly, not basely or in old wives' fashion?

Master. Will ye be flogged in your learning?

Pupil. We love rather to be beaten for learning's sake than to be ignorant; but we know that thou art a kindly man, who will not beat us unless we compel thee.

Master. I ask *thee*, then; what sayest thou? What is thy daily work?

Pupil. *I* am a professional monk, and I shall sing daily my seven services with the brethren, and am busy with reading and psalmody; yet in the mean time I would fain learn to speak in the Latin tongue.

Master. And these thy fellows, what know they?

Pupil. Some are ploughers, others shepherds, some are cowherds and some also are hunters, fishers, fowlers; some are merchants or cobblers or salters or bakers in this place.

[Each one then describes his own daily occupation, the monk comes last of all, adding, 'and now we stand here before thee, ready to hear what thou wilt say to us.']

Master. When will ye sing vespers or compline?

Pupil. When the time is come.

Master. Hast thou been beaten [in the monastery] to-day?

Pupil. No, for I kept myself cautiously.

Master. And thy fellows?

Pupil. Why dost thou question me of this matter? I dare not reveal our secrets unto thee; each knoweth in his own heart whether he hath been beaten or not . . .

Master. Where sleepest thou?

Pupil. In the dormitory, with the brethren.

Master. Who waketh thee for the night-services?

Pupil. Sometimes I hear the bell and arise; but sometimes my master arouseth me harshly with the rod — Aelfric, *Dialogues*, translated by G.G. Coulton.

Desire for Religion and Literature Had Declined in the Saxons Before the Normans Came

The clergy, contented with a very slight degree of learning, could scarcely stammer out the words of the sacraments; and a person who understood grammar was an object of wonder and astonishment. The monks mocked the rule of their Order by fine vestments, and the use of every kind of food. The nobility, given up to luxury and wantonness, went not to church in the morning after the manner of Christians, but merely, in a careless manner, heard Matins and Mass from a hurrying priest in their chambers, amid the blandishments of their wives. The commonalty, left unprotected, became a prey to the most powerful, who amassed fortunes, either by seizing on their property, or by selling their persons into foreign countries; although it be an innate quality of this people, to be more inclined to revelling than to the accumulation of wealth. There was one custom, repugnant to nature, which they adopted; namely, to sell their female servants, when pregnant by them and after they had satisfied their lust, either to public prostitution, or to foreign slavery. Drinking in parties was a universal practice, in which occupation they passed entire nights as well as days. They consumed their whole substance in mean and despicable houses; unlike the Normans and French, who, in noble and splendid mansions, lived with frugality. The vices attendant on drunkenness, which enervate the human mind, followed — William of Malmesbury, *De Gestis Regum*.

6 The Arts

The Funeral of Scyld Shefing, King of the Danes

From this we can learn how an English king of the Heroic Age was buried.

At the hour shaped for him Scyld departed,
the many-strengthened moved into his Master's keeping.

They carried him out to the current sea,
his sworn arms-fellows, as he himself had asked
while he wielded by his words, Ward of the Scyldings,
beloved folk-founder; long had he ruled.

A boat with a ringed neck rode in the haven,
icy, out-eager, the aetheling's vessel,
and there they laid out their lord and master,
dealer of wound gold, in the waist of the ship,
in majesty by the mast.
          A mound of treasures
from far countries was fetched aboard her,
and it is said that no boat was ever more bravely fitted out
with the weapons of a warrior, war accoutrement,
bills and byrnies; on his breast were set
treasures & trappings to travel with him
on his far faring into the flood's sway.

This hoard was not less great than the gifts he had
from those who sent him, on the sill of life,
over seas, alone, a small child.

High over head they hoisted and fixed
a gold *signum*; gave him to the flood,
let the seas take him, with sour hearts
and mourning moods. Men have not the knowledge
to say with any truth — however tall beneath the heavens,
however much listened to — who unloaded that boat.

Beowulf, translated by Michael Alexander in
The Earliest English Poems.

Hymn to the Creator by Caedmon

This is the only authentic part of his work to survive. It appeared in Latin in Bede's Historia Ecclesiastica Gentis Anglorum. *The translation below is by Professor Charles W. Kennedy.*

It is meet that we worship   the Warden of Heaven,
The might of the Maker,   His purpose of mind,
The Glory-Father's work   when all of His wonders
Eternal God   made a beginning.
He earliest established   for earth's children
Heaven for a roof,   the Holy Shaper;
Then Mankind's Warden   created the world,
Eternal Monarch,   making for men
Land to live on,   Almighty Lord!

Early English Christian Poetry,
translated by C.W. Kennedy.

From *Elene* by Cynewulf

This, his most famous poem, tells the story of the discovery of the true Cross by the Empress Helena Augusta, the mother of Constantine the Great. The translation is by Professor Charles W. Kennedy.

The Lady's departure   was plain to see
As she moved with her train   to the tumbling breakers.
Many a stately man   stood on the shore
Of the Wendel-sea.   Swiftly they hurried
Over the border-paths,   band after band.
They loaded the vessels   with buckler and lance,
With men in byrnies,   with battle-sarks,
With man and maid.   O'er the sea-monsters' home
they drove their foaming   deep-flanked ships.

Early English Christian Poetry,
translated by C.W. Kennedy.

In Praise of the Father *Altus Prosator*

'According to the traditions of the period, *c.* 565, it was composed by
Columba as a hymn of thanks and praise while he was grinding grain in
the mill on Iona. Shortly after emissaries came with rich gifts from
Pope Gregory. In return Columba gave them the text of the poem as a
gift for Gregory' — Harold Isbell.

The Most High, First Begetter,
Ancient of Days, Unbegotten:
he was without source,
primordial, unbounded;
throughout the span of ages
unending he is and will be.
With him is the only-begotten
Christ and the Holy Spirit
together eternal in the
unbroken glory of the godhead.
We do not present three gods,
rather we say that God is one
while we preserve our faith
in three most glorious persons.

In perfection did he create
the angels — orders and archangels
of every dominion and throne
and of every power and strength —
so that the goodness and
majesty of the Trinity
would not be idle
in any gift but
rather be surrounded
by heavenly beings who reveal
gifts greater than anything
words can ever describe.

From the apex of the Kingdom
of Heaven, from the paramount
brightness of the angelic ranks,
from the comeliness of his form
there fell, by excessive pride
Lucifer, whom God had made.

In the same mournful fall
of the author of vanity
and persistent envy
there went the apostate angels
while all the others remained
in the dignity of their dominions.

The great, most hideous dragon,
who was both terrible and old,
was also the slippery serpent
more knowing than all
the ferocious beasts and things
living on the earth.
He took with himself
into the pit of infernal life
and imprisonment, a third of the stars
who had given up the true light
and were evicted
by force from paradise.

The Most High, because he foresaw
the design and harmony of the world,
made the heavens and the earth.
He fashioned water and the sea,
as well as herbs producing seed;
the trees growing in groves
the sun, the moon and the stars,
fire and all things needed;
birds, fish, cattle,
beasts and all living things.
Finally, as he had planned, he made
the first man to rule creation . . .

St Columba. From *The Last Poets of Imperial Rome*,
translated by Harold Isbell.

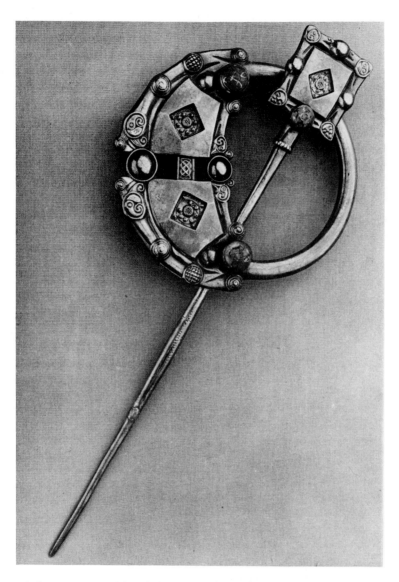

16. Silver brooch with gold insets in the terminals, Killamery, Co. Kilkenny, Ireland. Eighth century.

Tell Me, Broom Wizard

Broom gave power of all kinds.

'Tell me, broom wizard, tell me,
Teach me what to do,
To make my husband love me:
Tell me, broom wizard, do!'

'Silent tongue and still
Shall bring you all your will.'

From *Medieval English Verse*, translated by Brian Stone.

Senility

Before I was bent-backed, I was eloquent of speech,
my wonderful deeds were admired; the men of
Argoed always supported me.

Before I was bent-backed, I was bold; I was
welcomed in the drinking-hall of Powys, the
paradise of Wales.

Before I was bent-backed, I was handsome,
my spear was in the van, it drew first blood —
I am crooked, I am sad, I am wretched.

Wooden staff, it is Autumn, the bracken is red,
the stubble is yellow; I have given up what
I love.

Wooden staff, it is Winter, men are talkative over
the drink; no one visits my bedside.

Wooden staff, it is Spring, the cuckoos are
brown [female, slight reddish brown], there is light
at the evening meal; no girl loves me.

Wooden staff, it is early Summer, the furrow is
red, the young corn is curly; it grieves me
to look at your crook.

Wooden staff, knotty stick, support the yearning
old man, Llywarch, the perpetual babbler . . .
Boisterous is the wind, white is the hue of the
edge of the wood; the stag is emboldened, the

hill is bleak; feeble is the old man, slowly he moves . . .

What I have loved from boyhood I now hate —
a girl, a stranger, and a grey horse; indeed
I am not fit for them.

The four things I have most hated ever have
met together in one place; coughing and old
age, sickness and sorrow.

I am old, I am lonely, I am shapeless and cold
after my honoured couch; I am wretched, I am
bent in three.

I am bent in three and old, I am peevish and
giddy, I am silly, I am cantankerous;
those who loved me love me not.

Girls do not love me, no one visits me, I
cannot move about; ah, Death, why does it
not come for me!

Neither sleep nor joy come to me after the
slaying of Llawr and Gwen; I am an
irritable carcass, I am old.

A wretched fate was fated for Llywarch ever
since the night he was born — long toil without
relief from weariness.

> Welsh; attributed to 'Llywarch Hen'; ninth century.

Tradition says that Llywarch the Aged lived in the sixth century but
I. Williams, *Canu Llywarch Hen*, has shown that this poem belongs to
the ninth century. Llawr and Gwen were two of his many sons — from
A Celtic Miscellany, translated by Kenneth Hurlstone Jackson.

The Battle of Brunanburh

*The poem celebrates a victory won in 937 by King Athelstan against
Constantine, King of Scotland, who led a Scottish, Scandinavian and
British army.*

In this year king Athelstan, lord of warriors,
Ring-giver of men, with his brother prince Edmund,
Won undying glory with the edges of swords,
In warfare around *Brunanburh*.

With their hammered blades, the sons of Edward
Clove the shield-wall and hacked the linden bucklers,
As was instinctive in them, from their ancestry,
To defend their land, their treasures and their homes,
In frequent battle against each enemy.
The foemen were laid low: the Scots
And the host from the ships fell doomed. The field
Grew dark with the blood of men after the sun,
That glorious luminary, God's bright candle,
Rose high in the morning above the horizon,
Until the noble being of the Lord Eternal
Sank to its rest. There lay many a warrior
Of the men of the North, torn by spears,
Shot o'er his shield; likewise many a Scot
Sated with battle, lay lifeless.
All through the day the West Saxons in troops
Pressed on in pursuit of the hostile peoples,
Fiercely, with swords sharpened on grindstone,
They cut down the fugitives as they fled.
Nor did the Mercians refuse hard fighting
To any of Anlaf's warriors, who invaded
Our land across the tossing waters,
In the ship's bosom, to meet their doom
In the fight. Five young kings,
Stretched lifeless by the swords,
Lay on the field, likewise seven
Of Anlaf's jarls, and a countless host
Of seamen and Scots. There the prince
Of Norsemen, compelled by necessity,
Was forced to flee to the prow of his ship
With a handful of men. In haste the ship
Was launched, and the king fled hence,
Over the waters grey, to save his life.
    There, likewise, the agèd Constantine,
The grey-haired warrior, set off in flight,
North to his native land. No cause
Had he to exult in that clash of swords,
Bereaved of his kinsmen, robbed of his friends
On the field of battle, by violence deprived
Of them in the struggle. On the place of slaughter
He left his young son, mangled by wounds,

Received in the fight. No need to exult
In that clash of blades had the grey-haired warrior,
That practised scoundrel, and no more had Anlaf
Need to gloat, amid the remnants of their host,
That they excelled in martial deeds
Where standards clashed, and spear met spear
And man fought man, upon a field
Where swords were crossed, when they in battle
Fought Edward's sons upon the fateful field.

    The sorry Norsemen who escaped the spears
Set out upon the sea of Ding, making for Dublin
O'er deep waters, in ships with nailèd sides,
Ashamed and shameless back to Ireland.

    Likewise the English king and the prince,
Brothers triumphant in war, together
Returned to their home, the land of Wessex.

    To enjoy the carnage, they left behind
The horn-beaked raven with dusky plumage,
And the hungry hawk of battle, the dun-coated
Eagle, who with white-tipped tail shared
The feast with the wolf, grey beast of the forest.

    Never before in this island, as the books
Of ancient historians tell us, was an army
Put to greater slaughter by the sword
Since the time when Angles and Saxons landed,
Invading Britain across the wide seas
From the east, when warriors eager for fame,
Proud forgers of war, the Welsh overcame,
And won for themselves a kingdom.

Anglo-Saxon Chronicle,
translated by G.N. Garmonsway.

The Hermit's Hut

    ... I have a hut in the wood, none knows it but
my Lord; an ash tree this side, a hazel on the
other, a great tree on a mound encloses it ...

The stags of Druim Rolach leap out of its stream
of trim meadows; from them red Roighne can

be seen, noble Mucraimhe and Maenmhagh
[a plain round Longhrea, County Galway].

A little hidden lowly hut, which owns the
path-filled forest; will you go with me to see it?

A tree of apples of great bounty, huge; a seemly
crop from small-nutted branching green hazels,
in clusters like a fist.

Excellent fresh springs — a cup of water, splendid
to drink — they gush forth abundantly; yew
berries, bird-cherries . . .

Tame swine lie down around it, goats, young
pigs, wild swine, tall deer, does, a badger's
brood.

Fruits of rowan, black sloes of the dark
blackthorn; foods of whorts, spare berries.

A clutch of eggs, honey, produce of heath-peas,
God has sent it; sweet apples, red bog-berries,
whortleberries.

Beer with herbs, a patch of strawberries,
delicious abundance; haws, yew berries,
kernels of nuts.

A cup of mead from the goodly hazel-bush,
quickly served; brown acorns, manes of briar,
with fine blackberries.

In the summer with its pleasant, abundant
mantle, with good-tasting savour, there are
pignuts, wild marjoram, the cresses of the
stream — green purity!

A beautiful pine makes music to me, it is not
hired; through Christ, I fare no worse at
any time than you do.

Irish; author unknown; tenth century.
From *A Celtic Miscellany*,
translated by Kenneth Hurlstone Jackson.

17. Silver beakers from Denmark. Above, from Fejo, in a style inspired by southern England, *c.* 800. Below left, from Lejre, Zealand, tenth-century. Below right, from Jellinge, and it may be a chalice.

Gnomic Verses, *c.* 975

Frost shall freeze
                    fire eat wood
earth shall breed
                    ice shall bridge
water a shield wear.
                    One shall break
frost's fetters
                    free the grain
from wonder-lock
                    — One who all can.

Winter shall wane
                    fair weather come again
the sun-warmed summer!
                    The sound unstill
the deep dead wave
                    is darkest longest.
Holly shall to the pyre
                    hoard be scattered
when the body's numb
                    Name is best.

A king shall win
                    a queen with goods
beakers, bracelets.
                    Both must first
be kind with gifts.
                    Courage must wax
war-mood in the man,
                    the woman grow up
beloved among her people,
                    be light of mood
hold close a rune-word
                    be roomy-hearted
at hoard-share & horse-giving.

                    When the hall drinks
she shall always & everywhere
                    before any company

greet first
>   the father of aethelings
with the first draught
>   — deft to his hand she
holds the horn —
>   and when they are at home together
know the right way
>   to run their household.

The ship must be nailed
>   the shield framed
from the light linden.
>   But how loving the welcome
of the Frisian wife
>   when floats offshore
the keel come home again!

>   She calls him within walls,
her own husband
>   — hull's at anchor! —
washes salt-stains
>   from his stiff shirt
brings out clothes
>   clean & fresh
for her lord on land again.
>   Love's need is met.

> From *The Exeter Book*, authorised by King Alfred,
> translated by Michael Alexander.

The Ruin

'The Anglo-Saxons usually referred to Roman ruins as "the work of Giants".' This city is most probably Aquae Sulis, the Roman Bath. The poem comes from The Exeter Book, *975.*

Well-wrought this wall: Weirds [the Fates] broke it.
The stronghold burst . . .
Snapped rooftrees, towers fallen,
the work of the Giants, the stonesmiths,
mouldereth.

Rime scoureth gatetowers
rime on mortar.

Shattered the showershields, roofs ruined,
age under-ate them.
                    And the wielders & wrights?
Earthgrip holds them — gone, long gone,
fast in gravesgrasp while fifty fathers
and sons have passed.
                    Wall stood
grey lichen, red stone, kings fell often,
stood under storms, high arch crashed —
stands yet the wallstone, hacked by weapons
by files grim-ground . . .
. . . shone the old skilled work
. . . sank to loam-crust.

Mood quickened mind, and a man of wit,
cunning in rings, bound bravely the wallbase
with iron, a wonder.

Bright were the buildings, halls where springs ran,
high, horngabled, much throng-noise;
these many meadhalls men filled
with loud cheerfulness: Weird changed that.

Came days of pestilence, on all sides men fell dead,
death fetched off the flower of the people;
where they stood to fight, waste places
and on the acropolis, ruins.

                    Hosts who would build again
shrank to the earth. Therefore all these courts dreary
and that red arch twisteth tiles,
wryeth from roof-ridge, reacheth groundwards . . .
Broken blocks . . .

                    There once many a man
mood-glad, gold bright, of gleams garnished,
flushed with wine-pride, flashing war-gear,
gazed on wrought gemstones, on gold, on silver,
on wealth held and hoarded, on light-filled amber,
on this bright burg of broad dominion.

Stood stone houses; wide streams welled
hot from source, and a wall all caught
in its bright bosom, that the baths were
hot at hall's hearth; that was fitting . . .
. . .

Thence hot streams, loosed, ran over hoar stone
unto the ring-tank . . .
    . . . It is a kingly thing
    . . . city. . .

From *The Earliest English Poems*,
translated by Michael Alexander.

7 Sports and Pastimes

Greyhounds in Saxon Times

*In a metrical romance, called Sir Eglamore, a princess tells the knights,
that if he was inclined to hunt, she would, as a mark of her favour, give
him a splendid greyhound, so swift that no deer could escape from his
pursuit.*

Syr yf be an huntynge founde,
I shall you gyve a good greyhounde
That is dunne as a doo:
For as I am trewe gentylwoman,
There was never deer that he at ran,
There myght yscape him fro.

From Garrick's Collection of Old Plays, K vol. 10.

One Enjoys Rare Sport

One can play the harp with his hands; he has the cunning of quick
movements on the instrument. One is a swift runner; one a straight
shooter; one skilled in songs; one swift on the land, fleet of foot. One
guides the prow on the yellow wave; the leader of the host knows the
watery path over the vast sea, when mighty mariners with nimble
strength wield the oars by the ship. One is skilled in swimming; one an
artful workman in gold and gems when a protector of men bids him
set a jewel with splendour. One, a cunning smith, can make many weapons for use in war, when he shapes a helmet or short sword or corslet,
gleaming blade or the round shield; he can join them firmly against the
flying spear. One is pious and charitable, virtuous in his ways. One is a
nimble servant in the mead hall. One is well versed in horses, learned in
the arts of steeds. One with strong heart patiently endures what he
must needs. One knows laws where men seek counsel together. One is
clever at chess. One is witty at the wine-drinking, a good lord of the
beer. One is a builder, good at raising a dwelling. One is an army leader,

a bold general. One is a councillor. One is a servant with his lord, the
more bold at need. One has power to endure, a steadfast mind. One is
a fowler, skilled with the hawk. One is daring on horseback. One is very
swift, enjoys rare sport, the faculty of mirthful deeds before men,
sprightly and agile — from *The Arts of Men* in *The Exeter Book, c.* 975,
translated by R.K. Gordon.

18. This illustration of Saxon Gleemen is taken from an eighth-century
manuscript. The two men are dancing to the music of the horn and the
trumpet.

Skill at the Dicing-Board

Thus mighty God variously bestows, grants, and assigns to all over the
face of the earth, and orders their destinies; to one wealth; to one a
portion of suffering; to one joy in youth; to one success in war, mighty
war-play; to one a blow or stroke, radiant glory; to one skill at the
dicing-board, cunning at chess; some scribes become wise. For one a
wondrous gift is wrought by goldsmith's work; full often he hardens and
well adorns the corslet of the king of Britain, and he gives him broad
lands as a guerdon; gladly he receives it. One shall gladden men gathered
together, delight those sitting on the benches at the beer where the joy
of the drinkers is great. One shall sit at his lord's feet with his harp,

receive treasure and ever swiftly sweep the strings, let the plectrum, which leaps, sound aloud, the nail with its melody; great is the desire for him. One shall tame the wild bird in its pride, the hawk on the hand, till the falcon grows gentle. He puts foot-rings upon it, feeds it thus in fetters, proud of its plumage, wearies the swift flier with little food, till the foreign bird grows subject to his food giver in garb and act, and trained to the youth's hand — from *The Fates of Men* in *The Exeter Book*, *c.* 975, translated by R.K. Gordon.

19. The juggler is accompanied by the music from an instrument resembling the violin. They are Saxon Gleemen, two of many figures in an eighth-century manuscript in which the illumination is placed as frontispiece to the Psalms of David.

8 Health

How to Buy Off a Fast, *c.* 750

If anyone from illness or softness cannot undergo fasting and austerity, it is lawful for him to buy off his fast by piety and his worldly possessions. If accordingly he is rich let him give 30s. for 12 months fast. If he is not so wealthy let him give 20s. If he is less wealthy still let him give 10s. Finally if he be a poor man who cannot give 10s. let him give 3s. For a rich man can more easily give 30s., than a poor man can give 3s. A lawful shilling is always 12 pennies. Alms of this kind can be paid in three ways. One is that they be laid upon the altar of God; another is that a man can be bought from slavery and then set free; a third is, that they be distributed to God's poor — Penitential of Archbishop Ecgbert (735-66), B. Thorpe, *Ancient Laws and Institutes of England.*

A Charm with Yarrow

I will pick the smooth yarrow [a herb, milfoil]
that my figure may be more elegant, that
my lips may be warmer, that my voice may be
more cheerful; may my voice be like a
sunbeam, may my lips be like the juice of
the strawberries.

May I be an island in the sea, may I be a
hill on the land, may I be a star when
the moon wanes, may I be a staff to the
weak one: I shall wound every man, no
man shall wound me.

> Scottish Gaelic; traditional folk charm.
> From *A Celtic Miscellany,* translated
> by Kenneth Hurlstone Jackson.

Charms

Against Stomach-ache

Against stomach-ache and pain in the abdomen. When you see a dung-beetle throw up earth, catch it between your hands together with the heap. Wave it vigorously with your hands and say three times:

Remedium facio ad ventris dolorem.

Then throw away the beetle over your back and take care that you do not look after it.

When a man's stomach or abdomen pains him, catch the belly between your hands.
He will soon be better.
For twelve months you may do so after catching the beetle.

Against Dysentery

This letter was brought by an angel to Rome, when they were sorely afflicted with dysentery. Write this on parchment so long that it can go round the head, and hang it on the neck of the man who is in need of it.

He will soon be better.

Ranmigan. adonai. eltheos. mur. O ineffabile. Omiginan. midanmian. misane. dimas. mode. mida. mamagartem. Orta min. sigmone. beronice. irritas. venas quasi dulap. fervor. fruxantis. sanguinis. siccatur. fla. fracta. frigula. mirgui. etsihdon. segulta. frautantur. in arno. midoninis. abar vetho. sydone multo. sacculo. pp. pppp sother sother.

Miserere mei deus deus mini deus mi.

AΩNΥ Alleluiah. Alleluiah — fròm G. Storms, *Anglo-Saxon Magic.*

Against a Dwarf, a Convulsive Disease, in the Tenth Century

You must take seven little wafers, such as one uses in worship, and write these words on each wafer: Maximianus, Malchus, Johannes, Martinianus, Dionysious, Constantinus, Serapion. Then afterwards you must sing the charm which is given below, first into the left ear, then into the right ear, then over the man's head. And then let a maiden go to him and hang it upon his neck, and do this for three days; he will straightway be better.

Here came a spider creature stalking in;
He had his dress in his hand.
He said that thou wert his steed.

He puts his bonds on thy neck.
They began to sail from the land.
As soon as they left the land,
They began then to cool.
Then came the beast's sister stalking in,
Then she made an end and swore these oaths:
That this should never hurt the sick,
Nor him who could acquire this charm,
Nor him who could chant this charm.
Amen, fiat.

From *Anglo-Saxon Poetry*, translated
by R.K. Gordon.

20. This illustration is taken from an eighth-century manuscript. The archer with his dog is hunting wild deer; the other is shooting at birds; he carries four in his girdle.

Nine Herbs Charm (date unknown)

Forget not, Mugwort, what thou didst reveal,
What thou didst prepare at Regenmeld.
Thou hast strength against three and against thirty,
Thou hast strength against poison and against infection,
Thou hast strength against the foe who fares through the land.

And thou, Plantain, mother of herbs,
Open from the east, mighty within,
Over thee chariots creaked, over thee queens rode,
Over thee brides made outcry, over thee bulls gnashed their teeth.

All these thou didst withstand and resist;
So mayest thou withstand poison and infection,
And the foe who fares through the land.

This herb is called Stime; it grew on a stone,
It resists poison, it fights pain.
It is called harsh, it fights against poison.
This is the herb that strove against the snake;
This has strength against poison, this has strength against infection,
This has strength against the foe who fares through the land.

Now, Cock's-spur Grass, conquer the greater poisons,
        though thou art the lesser;
Thou, the mightier, vanquish the lesser until he is cured of both.

Remember, Mayweed, what thou didst reveal,
What thou didst bring to pass at Alorford:
That he never yielded his life because of infection,
After Mayweed was dressed for his food.

This is the herb which is called Wergulu;
The seal sent this over the back of the ocean
To heal the hurt of other poison.

These nine sprouts against nine poisons.

A snake came crawling, it bit a man.
Then Woden took nine glory-twigs,
Smote the serpent so that it flew into nine parts.
There Apple brought this to pass against poison,
That she nevermore would enter her house.

Thyme and Fennel, a pair great in power,
The Wise Lord, holy in heaven,
Wrought these herbs while He hung on the cross;
He placed and put them in the seven worlds

To aid all, poor and rich.
It stands against pain, resists the venom,
It has power against three and against thirty,
Against a fiend's hand and against sudden trick,
Against witchcraft of vile creatures.

Now these nine herbs avail against nine evil spirits,
Against nine poisons and against nine infectious diseases . . .
If any poison comes flying from the east or any comes from the
    north,
Or any from the west upon the people.

Christ stood over disease of every kind.
I alone know running water, and the nine serpents heed it;
May all pastures now spring up with herbs,
The sea, all salt water, be destroyed,
When I blow this poison from thee.

Mugwort, plantain which is open eastward, lamb's cress [wergulu?],
cock's-spur grass, mayweed, nettle [stime], crab-apple, thyme and
fennel, old soap; crush the herbs to dust, mix with soap and with the
apple's juice. Make a paste of water and of ashes; take fennel, boil it
in the paste and bathe with egg-mixture, either before or after he puts
on the salve. Sing that charm on each of the herbs: thrice before he
works them together and on the apple likewise; and sing that same
charm into the man's mouth and into both his ears and into the wound
before he puts on the salve — from *Anglo-Saxon Poetry*, translated by
R.K. Gordon.

Against Wens in the Tenth Century

Wen, wen, little wen,
Here thou shalt not build, nor have any abode.
But thou must pass forth to the hill hard by,
Where thou hast a brother in misery.
He shall lay a leaf at thy head.

Under the foot of the wolf, under the wing of the eagle,
Under the claw of the eagle, ever mayest thou fade,
Shrivel as coal on the hearth,
Shrink as muck in the wall,
And waste away like water in a bucket.
Become as small as a grain of linseed,
And far smaller also than a hand-worm's hip-bone,
And become even so small that thou become naught

From *Anglo-Saxon Poetry*, translated
by R.K. Gordon.

Anglo-Saxon Remedies from Leech-Books

Against lice: pound in ale, oak-rind and a little worm-wood; give to the lousy one to drink.

Against lice: quicksilver and old butter, one penny weight of quicksilver and two of butter; mingle all together in a brazen vessel.

In case a man be a lunatic; take skin of a mere-swine or porpoise, work it into a whip, swinge the man therewith, soon he will be well. Amen.

If thou be not able to staunch a blood-letting incision, take new horse's dung, dry it in the sun, rub it to dust thoroughly well, lay the dust very thick on a linen cloth; wrap up the wound with that [this could result in tetanus.]

Leechdoms, Wortconning and Starcraft of Early England,
Rolls Series.

21. A Saxon chieftain with his huntsmen and hounds pursuing wild swine in a forest; taken from a manuscript-painting of the ninth century.

9 Work and Payments

Enclosed and Open Fields, *c.* 700

A 'ceorl's' close [enclosed plot of land] ought to be fenced winter and summer. If it be unfenced, and his neighbour's cattle stray in through his own gap, he shall have nothing from the cattle: let him drive it out and bear the damage. . . .

If 'ceorls' have a common meadow, or other partible land to fence, and some have fenced their part, some have not, and eat up their common corn or grass; let those go who own the gap, and compensate to the others, who have fenced their part, the damage which there may be done, and let them demand such justice on the cattle as it may be right. But if there be a beast which breaks hedges and goes in everywhere, and he who owns it will not or cannot restrain it; let him who finds it in his field take it and slay it, and let the owner take its skin and flesh and forfeit the rest — Laws of Ine (688-94), 40 and 42, *Ancient Laws and Institutes of England.*

Hunting Whales and Walruses, Ninth Century

Ohthere told his lord King Aelfred, that he dwelt north-most of all the Northmen. He said that he dwelt in the land to the northward, along the West-Sea; he said, however, that that land is very long north from thence, but it is all waste, except in a few places, where the Finns here and there dwell, for hunting in the winter, and in the summer for fishing in that sea. He said that he was desirous to try, once on a time, how far that country extended due north, or whether any one lived to the north of the waste. He then went due north along the country, leaving all the way the waste land on the right, and the wide sea on the left, for three days: he was as far north as the whale-hunters go at the farthest. Then he proceeded in his course due north, as far as he could sail within another three days; then the land there inclined due east, or the sea into the

22. The Oseberg wagon. 'The decoration on the side and end of the wagon-body is executed in different styles' — Holger Arbman.

land, he knew not which, but he knew that he there waited for a west wind, or a little north, and sailed thence eastward along that land as far as he could sail in four days; then he had to wait for a due north wind, because the land there inclined due south, or the sea in on that land, he knew not which; he then sailed thence along the coast due south, as far as he could sail in five days. There lay a great river up in that land; they then turned up in that river, because they durst not sail on by that river, on account of hostility, because all that country was inhabited on the other side of that river; he had not before met with any land that was inhabited since he came from his own home; but all the way he had waste land on his right, except fishermen, fowlers, and hunters, all of whom were Finns, and he had constantly a wide sea to the left. The Beormas had well cultivated their country, but they did not dare to enter it; and the Terfinna land was all waste, except where hunters, fishers, or fowlers had taken up their quarters.

The Beormas told him many particulars both of their own land, and of the other lands lying around them; but he knew not what was true, because he did not see it himself; it seemed to him that the Finns and the Beormas spoke nearly one language. He went thither chiefly, in addition to seeing the country, on account of the walruses, because they have very noble bones in their teeth, some of those teeth they brought to the king: and their hides are good for ship-ropes. This whale is much less than other whales, it being not longer than seven ells; but in his own country is the best whale-hunting, there they are eight-and-forty ells long, and most of them fifty ells long; of these he said that he and five others had killed sixty in two days. He was a very wealthy man in those possessions in which their wealth consists, that is in wild deer. He had at the time he came to the king, six hundred unsold tame deer. These deer they call reindeer, of which there were six decoy reindeer, which are very valuable amongst the Finns, because they catch the wild reindeer with them — *Alfred's addition to his Anglo-Saxon version of Orosius,* translated by B. Thorpe.

Showing How the Danes Treated the English *c.* 900

But now, ere we proceed any further we will show what rule the Danes kept here in this realm before they were thus murdered, as in some books we find recorded. Whereas it is shown that the Danes compelled the husbandmen to till the ground and do all manner of labour and toil to be done about husbandry, the Danes lived upon the fruit and gains that came thereof. And when the husbandmen came home, then could they scarce have such sustenance of meats and drinks as fell for servants to have; so that, the Danes had all their commandments, eating and drinking of the best, where the silly man that was the owner, could hardly come to his fill of the worst.

Besides this, the common people were so oppressed by the Danes, that for fear and dread they called them in every house where any of them sojourned, Lord Dane, and if an Englishman and a Dane chanced to meet at any bridge or straight passage, the Englishman must stay till the Lord Dane were passed — Holinshed, *Chronicle,* I.

The Saxon Plough, 975

My nose is pointed downwards; I crawl along
and dig in the ground. I go as I am guided
by the gray enemy of the forest, and by my lord,

23. Anglo-Saxons digging, using spades
fitted with iron shoes.

who walks stooping, my guardian, at my tail,
pushes his way on the plain, lifts me and presses me on,
and sows in my track. Nose to ground, I move forwards,
having been brought from the wood, skilfully fastened together,
and carried on a wagon. I have many strange properties.
As I advance, on one side of me there is green,
while on the other my black track is clear.
Driven through my back there hangs under me
a well devised sharp weapon; another in my head,
firmly fixed and pointing forward, leans to the side,
so that I tear with my teeth, if from behind
he (that is, my lord) serves me well.

> Old English Riddle, translated by W.S. Mackie in
> *The Exeter Book*, pt ii, poems ix-xxxii,
> Early English Text Society, O.S.

A Bishop's Daily Work, Tenth Century

A bishop's daily work. That is rightly, his prayers first, and then his
book-work, reading or writing, teaching or learning; and his church
hours at the right time, always according to the things thereto befitting;

and washing the feet of the poor; and his alms-dealing; and the direction of work, where it may be needful. Good handycrafts are also befitting him, that crafts may be cultivated in his family [household], at least that no one too idle may dwell there. And it also well befits him, that at the 'gemōt' [assembly] he oft and frequently promulgate divine lore among the people with whom he then is — Saxon Institutes of Polity, Civil and Ecclesiastical, B. Thorpe, *Ancient Laws and Institutes of England.*

Workers Tell Us of Their Work, *c.* 990

[The Ploughman says:] 'I work hard; I go out at day break, driving the oxen to the field, and I yoke them to the plough. Be it never so stark winter I dare not linger at home for fear of my lord; but having yoked my oxen, and fastened share and coulter, every day I must plough a full acre or more. I have a boy driving the oxen with a goad-iron, who is hoarse with cold and shouting. And I do more also. I have to fill the oxen's bins with hay and water them, and take out their litter . . . mighty hard work it is, for I am not free.'

[The Shepherd says:] 'In the first of the morning I drive my sheep to their pasture and stand over them, in heat and in cold with my dogs, lest the wolves swallow them up; and I lead them back to their folds and milk them twice a day; and their folds I move; and I make cheese and butter, and I am true to my lord.'

[The Oxherd says:] 'When the ploughman unyokes the oxen, I lead them to pasture, and all night I stand over them, waking against thieves; and then again in the early morning I betake them well filled and watered, to the ploughman.'

[The king's Hunter says:] 'I braid nets and set them in fit places, and set my hounds to follow up the wild game, till they come unsuspecting to the net and are caught therein; and I slay them in the net. . . . With swift hounds I hunt down wild game. I take harts and boars, and bucks and roes, and sometimes hares. I give the king what I take, because I am his hunter. He clothes me well, and feeds me, and sometimes gives me a horse as an arm-ring that I may pursue my craft the more merrily.'

[The Fisher says:] 'I go on board my boat and cast my net into the river, and cast my angle and baits, and what they catch I take. I cast the unclean fish away and take me the clean for meat. The citizens buy my fish, I cannot catch as many as I could sell. Eels and pike, minnows and eel-pout, trout and lampreys. . . . In the sea I catch herrings and lax [salmon], porpoises, and sturgeon, oysters and crabs, mussels, periwinkles, sea-cockles, plaice and fluke [flounder], and lobsters and many of the like. . . . It is a perilous thing to catch a whale. It is pleasanter for me to go to the river with my boat than to go with many boats whale-hunting.'

[The Fowler says:] 'In many ways I trick the birds — sometimes with nets, with gins, with lime, with whistling, with a hawk, with traps.'

[The Merchant says:] 'I go aboard my ship with my goods, and I go over seas and sell my things, and buy precious things which are not produced in this country, and bring them hither to you . . . pall [brocade] and silk, precious gems and gold, various raiment, and dye-stuffs, wine and oil, ivory and mastling [brass-stone], copper and tin, sulphur and glass and the like, and I wish to sell them dearer here than I buy there, that I may get some profit wherewith I may feed myself and my wife and my sons' — *The Colloquies of Aelfric*, translated by B. Thorpe in *Analecta Anglo-Saxonica*.

The Carpenter's Tools Speak in a Debate

The shype ax seyd unto the wryght:
Mete and drynke I schall the plyght,
Clene hose and clene schone [shoes],
Gete them wer as euer thou kane . . .
Wherefore, seyd the belte,
With grete strokes I schalle hym pelte;
My mayster schall full welle thene,
Both to clothe [and] fede his men.
Ye, ye, seyd the twybylle [mortising axe],
Thou spekes euer ageyne skylle. . . .
Yis, yis, seyd the wymbylle [gimlet],
I ame als rounde as a thymbyll;
My maysters werke I wylle remembyre,
I schall crepe fast into the tymbyre,
And help my mayster within a stounde [hour]
To store his cofere with xx pounde. . . .
Than seyd the whetstone:
Thoff my mayster thryft be gone,

I schall hym helps within this yere
To gete hym xx merke clere;
Hys axes schall I make fulle scharpe,
That thei may lyghtly do ther werke;
To make my master a ryche man
I schall asey, If that I canne . . .

From a manuscript in the Bodleian Library, quoted in
C.F. Innocent, *Building Construction.*

Cattle, Tenth Century

If any one pursue the track of stolen cattle from one 'staeth' [a station on the boundary river] to another, then let him commit the tracing to the men of the country or show by some mark that it is rightfully pursued. Let him then take to it who owns the land, and have the inquiry to himself, and 9 days afterwards compensate for the cattle, or deposit an 'underwed' [pledge] on that day, which shall be worth half as much again as the cattle; and in 9 days from that time let him redeem the 'wed' [pledge] by lawful payment. If it be said that the track is wrongfully pursued, then must he who traces the cattle lead to the 'staeth', and there himself one of six unchosen men, who are true, make oath that he according to folk-right [customary law] makes lawful claim on the land, as his cattle went thereup — Ordinance established by the English witan and the counsellors of the Welsh nation established among the 'Dunsetas', B. Thorpe, *Ancient Laws and Institutes of England.*

A Ceorl Usually Held One Hide (about 120 acres)

At Hurstbourne Priors in Hampshire, about 1030, ceorls had to render for every hide:

40 pence at the autumnal equinox, and 6 church 'mittan' of ale and 3 sesters of wheat for bread, and they must plough 3 acres in their own time, and sow them with their own seed, and bring it to the barn in their own time, and give 3 pounds of barley as rent, and mow half an acre of meadow as rent in their own time, and make it into a rick, and supply 4 fothers of split wood as rent, made into a stack in their own time, and

supply 16 poles of fencing as rent likewise in their own time, and at Easter they shall give 2 ewes with 2 lambs — and we reckon 2 young sheep to a full-grown sheep — and they must wash the sheep and shear them in their own time, and work as they are bidden every week except three — one at midwinter, the second at Easter, the third at the Rogation Days — *English Historical Documents*, Vol. I.

Allowances Due to Various Persons in the Reign of Cnut, 1016-1035

The *Swineherd* who looks after the herd of pigs belonging to the lord and is only a slave may have the stypig and its pluck [heart, liver, and lungs] when he has carefully prepared the bacon and any other rights which by law pertain to slaves.

A *Slave-woman* is entitled to eight pounds of corn for food, one sheep or three pennies for winter food, one sester [measure, about a pint] of beans for lenten fare, and in summer whey or one penny.

All *Slaves* are entitled to a Christmas feast and an Easter feast, and in harvest a handful of corn besides their dues.

The *Sowers* shall have one basketful of every kind of seed when he has sown all the seed well for a year.

The *Oxherd* is permitted to pasture two oxen or more with the herd belonging to his lord on the common with the sanction of his overseer . . .

The *Cowherd* may have the milk of a cow for seven nights after she has calved.

The *Shepherd's* due is that he may have twelve nights manure at Christmas and one lamb and the fleece of a bellwether and the milk of his flock for seven nights before the autumnal Equinox and throughout the Summer a cupful of buttermilk.

The *Goatherd* claims the milk of his flock after Martinmas day and previous to that his share of buttermilk and a yearling kid if he looks after his flock well.

The *Cheesemaker's* due is one hundred cheeses and to make butter for the lord's table she may have all the buttermilk except the shepherd's share.

The *Barn-man* is entitled to whatever corn falls at the door of the barn in harvest if his overseer grants it to him and he faithfully deserves it.

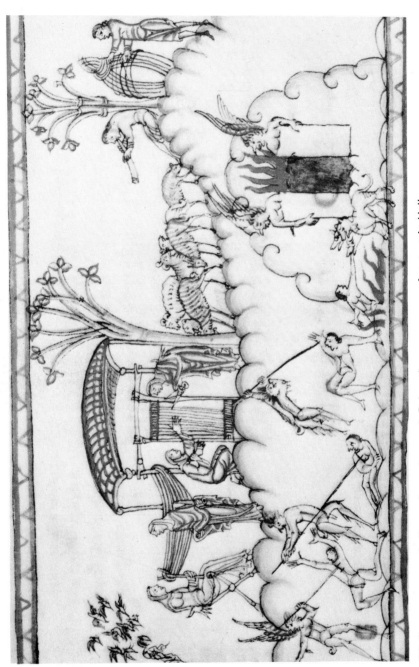

24. Saxon women winding and weaving wool. Below them are scenes of torture in Hell.

The *Beadle's* due is that he is on account of his office freer of work than other men; because he must be more often available. He is entitled to some piece of land for his work.

The *Woodward* is entitled to every tree blown down by the wind.

The *Hayward's* due is that he be rewarded in that part of the land adjoining the meadow; because he ought to know that if he does not guard this, any damage will be imputed to him. And if any portion of land is given him, according to public law it ought to be adjoining the meadow-land, so that in the event of cattle breaking through owing to his own carelessness his own land will be the first to suffer.

The laws and customs of estates are many and various as we have said before, and we do not lay down a general rule; but we note what is the custom in certain districts. If better customs are brought to our notice we will gladly approve and endeavour to hold by the customs of the people amongst whom we are then living — *Rectitudines Singularum Personarum*, translated from the Latin version in B. Thorpe, *Ancient Laws and Institutes*.

Dues from Various People in Cnut's Reign

The *Beekeeper*, if he hold a swarm of bees, etc. must pay according to the custom of the estate. In some places it is laid down that he pay five sesters [liquid measure for beer, wine etc. about a pint] of honey as rent . . .

The *Swineherd* paying pig-rent must supply his pigs for slaughter according to the custom of the locality. In many places it is decreed that every year he shall give fifteen pigs for killing, ten old and five young; he himself may keep what he has over and above this number — *Rectitudines Singularum Personarum*, translated from the Latin version in B. Thorpe, *Ancient Laws and Institutes*.

Tax-Collectors Killed by the People of Worcestershire in 1041

In this year Hardacnut, king of the English, sent his housecarls through all the provinces of his kingdom to collect the tax which he had imposed. Two of them, namely Feader and Thurstan, were killed on Monday, 4 May, by the people of Worcestershire and the citizens, in an upper

25. Builders at work.

room of a tower of the monastery of Worcester, to which they had fled to hide themselves when a riot had broken out.

Hence the king, moved to anger, sent there to avenge their slaying Thuri of the Midlanders, Leofric of the Mercians, Godwine of the West Saxons, Siward of the Northumbrians, Hrani of the *Magonsaete* [Herefordshire], and the other earls of the whole of England, and almost all his housecarls, with a great army, while Ælfric was still holding the bishopric of Worcester; ordering them to kill, if they could, all the men, to plunder and burn the city and to lay waste the whole province.

When the 12 November arrived, they began to lay waste both the city and the province, and did not cease to do so for four days; but they captured or killed few either of the citizens or of the men of the province, because, having notice of their coming, the people of the province had fled in all directions; a great number of the citizens, however, took refuge in a certain small island which is called Bevere, situated in the middle of the Severn, and having made a fortification, defended themselves manfully against their enemies until peace was restored and they were allowed to return home freely. Accordingly, on the fifth day, when the city had been burnt, everyone went off to his own parts with much booty, and the king's wrath was at once appeased.

Not long afterwards, Edward, the son of Ethelred, formerly king of the English, came from Normandy, where he had lived in exile for many years, to England, and being honourably received by his brother, King Hardacnut, remained in his court — Florence of Worcester, *Chronicle of Chronicles*, edited by B. Thorpe.

26. A reeve, steward or overseer for the lord of the manor, supervising the villeins reaping corn.

10 Religion

How the Picts Received the Faith of Christ, 565

In the year of our Lord 565, when Justin the Younger succeeded Justinian and ruled as Emperor of Rome, a priest and abbot named Columba, distinguished by his monastic habit and life, came from Ireland to Britain to preach the word of God in the provinces of the northern Picts, which are separated from those of the southern Picts by a range of steep and desolate mountains [the Grampians].

The southern Picts, who live on this side of the mountains, are said to have abandoned the errors of idolatry long before this date and accepted the true Faith through the preaching of Bishop Ninian [a native of North Wales], who had been regularly instructed in the mysteries of the Christian Faith in Rome. Ninian's own episcopal see, named after Saint Martin and famous for its stately church, is now held by the English, and it is here that his body and those of many saints lie at rest. The place belongs to the province of Bernicia [Northumberland] and is commonly known as *Candida Casa*, the White House [Whithorn, Galloway], because he built the church of stone, which was unusual, among the Britons.

Columba arrived in Britain in the ninth year of the reign of the powerful Pictish king, Bride son of Meilochon. He converted that people to the Faith of Christ by his preaching and example, and received from them the island of Iona on which to found a monastery. Iona is a small island, with an area of about five hides according to English reckoning, and his successors hold it to this day. It was here that Columba died and was buried at the age of seventy-seven, some thirty-two years after he had come into Britain to preach. Before he came to Britain, he had founded a noble monastery in Ireland known in the Scots language as *Dearmach*, the Field of Oaks [Durrow], because of the oak forest in which it stands. From both of these monasteries Columba's disciples went out and founded many others in Britain and Ireland; but the monastery on the isle of Iona, where his body lies, remains the chief of them all.

Iona is always ruled by an abbot in priest's orders, to whose authority the whole province, including the bishops, is subject, contrary to the
usual custom [the Celtic custom was for the abbot of a monastery to
exercise ecclesiastical jurisdiction over the *provincia*, while the bishop,
a member of the monastic community, was to exercise his episcopal
functions at the behest of the abbot]. This practice was established by
its first abbot Columba, who was not a bishop himself, but a priest and
monk. His life and sayings are said to have been recorded in writing
by his disciples. But whatever type of man he may have been, we know
for certain that he left successors distinguished for their purity of life,
their love of God, and their loyalty to the monastic rule.

In observing the great Feast of Easter they followed doubtful rules;
for being so isolated from the rest of the world, there was no one to
acquaint them with the synodical decrees about the keeping of Easter.
But they diligently followed whatever pure and devout customs they
learned in the prophets, the Gospels, and the writing of the Apostles.
They held to their own manner of keeping Easter for another 150 years,
until the year of our Lord 715 — Bede, *Historia Ecclesiastica Gentis
Anglorum*, translated by Leo Sherley-Price.

English Slaves in Rome, 575

Some of these youths then, carried from England for sale to Rome,
became the means of salvation of all their countrymen. For exciting the
attention of that city, by the beauty of their countenances and the
elegance of their features, it happened there, among others, the blessed
Gregory, at that time archdeacon of the Apostolical See, was present.
Admiring such an assemblage of grace in mortals, and at the same time
pitying their abject condition, as captives, he asked the standers-by, 'Of
what race are these? Whence come they?' They reply, 'By birth they are
Angles, by country are Deiri; [Deira a province of Northumbria], subjects of King Alla and Pagans.' Their concluding characteristic he accompanied with heartfelt sighs; to the others he elegantly alluded, saying,
'that these Angles, *Angel*-like, should be delivered from (*de*) *ira*, and
taught to sing *Alle-luia*.' Obtaining permission without delay from Pope
Benedict, the industry of this excellent man was all alive to enter on the
journey to convert them; and certainly his zeal would have completed
his intended labour, had not the mutinous love of his fellow-citizens
recalled him, already on his progress . . . His good intention, though

frustrated at this time, received afterwards during his pontificate an honourable termination – William of Malmesbury, *Chronicle*, I, iii, translated by J.A. Giles.

27. The monastery founded by St Columba on the island of Iona, *c.* 563. Became renowned centre of Celtic missions. On the right the Great Cross of Iona.

The Conversion of England to Christianity, 596

Augustine, the Servant of God, was sent by the blessed Pope Gregory into Britain to preach the Word of God to the barbarous nation of the Angles. For they, being blinded by Pagan superstitions, had destroyed all Christianity in that part of the Island which they occupied. But among some portions of the Britons, the faith of Christ still flourished which, having been introduced in the hundred and fifty-eighth year after the divine incarnation, was never wholly lost from among them.

On the Eastern side of Kent is the Isle of Thanet, on which the man of God, Augustine, and his companions, to the number, as it is reported of about forty men, landed and Augustine, sending interpreters to King Ethelbert, gave him notice that he had come from Rome, and that he was the bearer of excellent tidings, because he promised eternal joy in heaven to those who should obey him. The king, hearing this, came a few days afterwards to the island, and sitting down in the open air, invited Augustine and his companions to come there to a conference with him.

And they, being endowed with divine courage, came, bearing a cross for a standard, and a likeness of our Lord and Saviour depicted on a picture, and chanting litanies for their own salvation, and that of those for whom they had come. And when at the command of the king, they had sat down, they presented the Word of Life to him and to all who had come with him, and he replied saying. 'The things which you promise are beautiful but because they are new to me and doubtful I cannot at the moment give my assent to them, forsaking these things which I and my nation have so long preserved. But because you, being foreigners, have come hither from a great distance, and because you have been desirous to communicate to me the things which you yourselves believe to be true and excellent, we are not disposed to deal harshly with you. Nor do we prohibit you from winning over to the faith of your religion, all whom you can influence by preaching.'

Accordingly, he assigned them an abode in the City of Canterbury, which was the capital of his dominions, where they began to imitate the apostolic life of the primitive church, using continued prayers and fastings, and preaching the Word of God, and bathing all whom they could convince in the laver of salvation. And immediately many believed and were baptised.

On the east there was a church close to the city itself, which had been built in old time in honour of the blessed Martin, in which the Queen, the daughter of the King of France, by name Bertha, had been accustomed to pray, and in which these missionaries began also to meet together and preach and celebrate masses and baptise. And the king himself among them believed and was baptised. He also allotted to the doctors a habitation suitable to their degree in his own metropolis, the City of Canterbury, and he gave them what was necessary for them in particular — Matthew of Westminster, *Flowers of History*, X, translated by C.D. Yonge.

St Brendan's Vision of Hell

Brénainn; St Brendan, sixth-century Irish saint

However the Devil revealed the gate of Hell to Brénainn then. And Brénainn beheld that rough murky prison, full of stench, full of flame, full of filth, full of encampments of venomous demons, full of the weeping and shrieking and injury and pitiful cries and great wailings and lamentation and beating together of hands, of the tribes of sinners; and a dismal sorrowful life in kennels of torture, in prisons of fire, in streams of waves of everlasting fire, in a cup of eternal sorrow, in black dark sloughs, in chairs of mighty flame, in profusion of sorrow and death and torment and bonds and irresistible heavy combat, with the terrible yelling of the venomous demons; in the eternally dark, eternally cold, eternally stinking, eternally foul, eternally gloomy, eternally rough, eternally long, eternally melancholy, deadly, baneful, severe, fiery-haired dwelling place of the most hideous depths of Hell, on the slopes of mountains of everlasting fire, without stay, without rest; but troops of demons are dragging them into pitiful, grievous, rigid, fiery, dark, deep, hidden, empty, base, black, idle, filthy, antiquated, old and stinking, everlastingly quarrelsome, everlastingly pugnacious, everlastingly wearisome, everlastingly deadly, everlastingly tearful prisons; sharp, fierce, windy, full of wailing, screaming, complaining, and bitter crying; horrible.

There are curly, cruel, bold, big-headed maggots; and yellow, white, great-jawed monsters; fierce ravening lions; red, black, brown, devilish dragons; mighty treacherous tigers; inky bristly scorpions; red high-soaring hawks; rough sharp-beaked griffins; black hump-backed beetles; sharp snouted flies; bent bony-beaked wasps; heavy iron mallets; ancient old rough flails; sharp swords; red spears; black demons; stinking fires; streams of poison; cats scratching; dogs rending; hounds hunting; demons calling; fetid lakes; great sloughs; dark pits; deep gullies; high mountains; hard crags; a mustering of demons; a filthy camp; torture without cease; a ravenous swarm; frequent conflict; endless fighting; demons torturing; torment in abundance; a sorrowful life.

A place in which there are frosty, bitter, everlastingly fetid, wide-spread, wide-stretched, agitated, grievous, putrid, deliquescent, burning, bare, rapid, full-fiery streams; hard, rocky, sharp-headed, long, cold, deep, swampy little straits of the sea; bare burning plains; peaked rugged hills; hard verminous ravines; rough thorny moors; black fiery forests; filthy monster-infested roads; congealed stinking-billowed seas; huge iron spikes; black bitter waters; many extraordinary places; a dirty everlastingly-gloomy assembly; bitter wintry winds; frosty ever-lastingly-falling snow; red fiery blades; base dark faces; swift ravening demons; vast unheard-of tortures.

Then his followers asked Brénainn, 'Who are you talking to?' said they. Brénainn told them that it was the Devil who was talking to him; and told them a little of the tortures he had seen, as we have said, according as it has been found in the ancient writings of the Old Testament – Irish; author unknown; twelfth century. From *A Celtic Miscellany*, translated by Kenneth Hurlstone Jackson.

Gildas Attacks the Behaviour of the Stricter Monks in the Early Sixth Century

Abstinence from bodily foods without charity is useless. The real *meliores* [the stricter monks] are those who fast without ostentation . . . not those who think themselves superior because they refuse to eat meat . . . or to ride on a horse or in a carriage; for death enters into them by the windows of pride . . .

The *meliores* criticise brethren who do not follow their arrogant conceits . . . They eat bread by measure, and boast of it beyond measure; they drink water, and with it the cup of hatred. Their meals are dry dishes and backbiting . . . When they meditate their 'Great Principles' it is from contempt, not from love. They put the serf before his master, the mob before its king, lead before gold, iron before silver . . . They set fasting above charity, vigils above justice, their own conceits above concord, their cell above the church, severity above humility; in a word, they prefer man to God. It is not the Gospels they obey, but their own will, not the apostle but their own pride. They forget that the position of the stars in heaven is not equal, and that the offices of the angels are unequal – Gildas, in *Six Old English Chronicles*. From John Morris, *The Age of Arthur.*

The Last Words of St Columba, 597

These, my last words, I commend unto you, O my children, that ye shall preserve among yourselves unfeigned charity and mutual peace; and if ye observe this rule according to the example of the holy fathers, God, the Strengthener of the good, will help you; and I, dwelling with Him, will pray for you; and not only shall there be provided for you by Him the necessaries of the present life, but also there shall be given you the gifts of eternal good things prepared for them that keep the Divine Commandments — to the Brethren of All the Churches of his Order, from W. Reeves, *The Life of St Columba.*

Augustine Reaches Britain, Preaches in the Isle of Thanet Before King Ethelbert, 597

Reassured by the encouragement of the blessed father Gregory [the pope], Augustine and his fellow-servants of Christ resumed their work in the world of God, and arrived in Britain.

At this time the most powerful king there was Ethelbert, who reigned in Kent and whose domains extended northwards to the river Humber, which forms the boundary between the north and south Angles. To the east of Kent lies the large island of Thanet, which by English reckoning is six hundred hides [one hide the amount of land to support one family] in extent; it is separated from the mainland by a waterway about three furlongs broad called the Wantsum, which joins the sea at either end and is fordable only in two places.

It was here that God's servant Augustine landed with companions, who are said to have been forty in number. At the direction of blessed Pope Gregory, they had brought interpreters from among the Franks, and they sent these to Ethelbert, saying that they came from Rome bearing very glad news, which infallibly assured all who would receive it of eternal joy in heaven and an everlasting kingdom with the living and true God.

On receiving this message, the king ordered them to remain in the island where they had landed, and gave directions that they were to be provided with all necessaries until he should decide what action to take. For he had already heard of the Christian religion, having a Christian wife, of the Frankish royal house, named Bertha, whom he had received from her parents on condition that she should have freedom to hold and practise her faith unhindered with Bishop Liudhard, whom they had sent as her helper in the faith.

After some days, the king came to the island and, sitting down in the open air, summoned Augustine and his companions to an audience. But he took precautions that they should not approach him in a house; for he held an ancient superstition that, if they were practisers of magical arts, they might have opportunity to deceive and master him. But the monks were endowed with power from God, not from the Devil, and approached the king carrying a silver cross as their standard and the likeness of our Lord and Saviour painted on a board.

First of all they offered prayer to God, singing a litany for the eternal salvation both of themselves and of those to whom and for whose sake they had come. And when, at the king's command, they had sat down and preached the word of life to the king and his court, the king said, 'Your words and promises are fair indeed; but they are new and uncertain, and I cannot accept them and abandon the age-long beliefs that I have held together with the whole English nation. But since you have travelled far, and I can see that you are sincere in your desire to impart to us what you believe to be true and excellent, we will not harm you . . .'

The king then granted them a dwelling in the city of Canterbury, which was the chief city of all his realm, and in accordance with his promise he allowed them provisions and did not withdraw their freedom to preach.

Tradition says that as they approached the city, bearing the holy cross and the likeness of our great King and Lord Jesus Christ as was their custom, they sang in unison this litany: 'We pray Thee, O Lord, in all Thy mercy, that Thy wrath and anger may be turned away from this city and from Thy holy house, for we are sinners' — Bede, *Historia Ecclesiastica Gentis Anglorum*, translated by Leo Sherley-Price.

After the Deaths of the Kings Ethelbert and Saeberht, Their Successors Restored Idolatry, *c.* 616

But after the death of Ethelbert, when his son Aedbald had received the government of the kingdom, this proved very harmful to the still tender growth of the Church there. For he not only refused to accept the faith of Christ, but also was defiled with fornication of such a kind as, the

Apostle testifies, was unheard of even among the Gentiles, that one should have his father's wife. By both these crimes he gave occasion for those to return to their former vomit who, under the rule of his father, had accepted the laws of faith and chastity either for favour or fear of the king. Nor were the scourges of the heavenly severity lacking to punish and correct the unbelieving king; for he was seized by frequent attacks of madness, and possessed by an unclean spirit.

The storm of this disturbance was increased by the death of Saeberht, king of the East Saxons, who, when he sought the everlasting kingdom, left as heirs to a temporal kingdom for his three sons, who had remained heathen. They began immediately to practise openly the idolatry which during his lifetime they seemed to have left off a little, and freely to give permission to their subjects to worship idols. And when they saw the bishop, in celebrating the solemnities of the Mass in the church, give the Eucharist to the people, they said, as it is commonly reported, puffed up with ignorant folly: 'Why do you not give us also that white bread which you used to give to our father, Saba' — for thus they used to call him — 'and still continue to give to the people in church?' To whom he replied: 'If you will be washed in that font of salvation in which your father was washed, you can also be partakers of the holy bread of which he partook; but if you despise the laver [font] of life, by no means can you receive the bread of life.' And they said: 'We will not enter that font, because we know that we have no need of it, but yet we will be fed with that bread.'

And when they had been earnestly and often admonished by him, that it could on no account be, that anyone should share in the sacred oblation without the sacred purification, they finally were moved to anger and said: 'If you will not comply with us in so light a matter, as we request, you shall not stay any longer in our province.' And they expelled him, and ordered him to leave their kingdom with his followers.

Being expelled from there, he went to Kent, to confer with Laurence and Justus, his fellow-bishops, what should be done in that case. And they decided by common consent that it was better for them all to return to their own land and serve God there with a free mind, than to remain to no purpose among barbarians revolted from the faith. And thus Mellitus and Justus departed first and withdrew into the regions of Gaul, intending to await the issue of events there.

But the kings who had driven away from them the herald of the truth did not follow the worship of devils for very long with impunity. For they went out to battle against the nation of the Gewisse [West

Saxons] and all fell together, along with their army. Yet, the people whom they had turned to wickedness, although the authors of it had perished, could not be corrected and recalled to the simplicity of the faith and charity, that is in Christ — Bede's *Ecclesiastical History of the English Nation*. Translation of D. Whitelock partly based on that of J.A. Giles.

Part of a Letter of Pope Boniface V to King Edwin, *c*. 625

Here is a call to the observance of the true faith, and to the ending of all idolatry.

We suppose that your highness, because of the proximity of place, has become thoroughly acquainted with what the mercy of the redeemer has wrought in the enlightenment of our glorious son, King Audubald, and the peoples subject to him. We therefore trust with assured hope that by heavenly long-suffering this wonderful gift is being bestowed upon you; since indeed we have learned that your illustrious consort, who is discerned to be part of your body, has been enlightened with the reward of eternity through the regeneration of holy baptism — *English Historical Documents*, Vol. I.

The Spiritual Conversion of Northumbria, 627

[King Edwin] listened [to Paulinus] and replied that he wished to receive the faith as explained and that it was his duty. He would discuss it with his chief friends and advisers so that if they agreed they should all be consecrated together in Christ, the Fountain of Life. Paulinus consented and he acted accordingly. He asked each of the wise men at a council his views on the New Teaching and Preaching of a novel religion.

Coifi answered before any of his subordinate priests: 'Examine, O King, this preaching, yourself, but I am telling the whole truth when I confess that I find our former beliefs are unprofitable and useless. None of your subjects was more meticulous than I in the worship of our gods but many had more royal favours than I with more promotion and they gain their ends more; but if the gods were any good they would back up me as I served them better. If, therefore, reflexion leads you to consider the New Preaching of greater virtue and efficacy, let us accept them with no more ado.'

Another noble saw his wisdom and added: 'The life of man, O King, compared with the time of which we know not, is like the flight of a sparrow through the hall. There you sit at meat with your chieftains and servants in winter time with a fire blazing in the midst and rain and storm blustering outside and in it flies through one door and quickly out of the other. While it is within it is not touched by the winter storm, but after a little while of calm it vanishes from your sight into the winter again. Thus we see the life of man for a span, but what came before or what follows after we know not. If the New Teaching brings surer knowledge, surely it should be followed.' The other elders and counsellors of the king were prompted by God to speak likewise.

Coifi asked to hear Paulinus more carefully on his God. The king commanded and he did this and when he had listened he cried 'I long knew that our religion was meaningless, for the more I sought truth therein the less I found it. Now I make public confession that truth shines in this preaching and can give us life, salvation and eternal bliss. I propose, O King, that we straightway curse and burn the shrines and altars which we have honoured without profit.' To cut a long story short, the king publicly licensed the mission of Paulinus, renounced his idolatry and accepted Christianity. He asked the Chief Priest who should first desecrate the altars and shrines of the idols with their precincts and he replied 'I. Who better than I who ignorantly worshipped them, for an example to all by the wisdom God has given me?' Spurning superstition he straightway asked the king for arms and a stallion. He mounted and rode to destroy the idols. It had been unlawful for a priest to carry arms or ride, save on a mare. With sword girded, he grasped a lance, mounted the king's stallion and hurried to the idols. The mob gazed and thought him possessed. Without a pause he charged to the shrine, cast in his lance and desecrated it. Glad in the knowledge of the true God he bade his comrades burn the shrine and its precincts. The very spot is still shown, near York — translated from *Venerabilis Baedae Opera Historica.*

The Monastery on Lindisfarne Shows the Simplicity of the Celtic Ideal, Seventh Century

... there were very few houses found there, except the church, only those, that is, without which no civilized way of living could exist. They [the monks] had no money, but only cattle. For if they received any money from the rich, they gave it immediately to the poor. For there was no need either to collect money or to provide houses for the entertainment of the great men of the world, for they never came to the church except only to pray and to hear the word of God. The king himself, when occasion required, used to come with only five or six thegns, and to depart when he had performed his devotions in church. But if by chance it happened that they took a repast there, they were content with the simple and daily food of the brothers, and demanded nothing more. For at that time the whole care of those teachers was to serve God, not the world; their whole care was to feed the soul, and not the belly — Bede, *Historia Ecclesiastica Gentis Anglorum.*

The Influence of the Church

Theodore arrived at his church the second year after his consecration, on Sunday, the 27th of May 669. . . Soon after, he visited all the island, wherever the tribes of the Angles inhabited, for he was willingly entertained and heard by all persons; and everywhere attended and assisted by Hadrian he taught the right rule of life and the Canonical custom of celebrating Easter. This was the first Archbishop whom all the English Church obeyed.

And forasmuch as both of them were, as has been said before, well read both in sacred and in secular literature, they gathered a crowd of disciples, and there daily flowed from them rivers of knowledge to water the hearts of their hearers; and together with the books of holy writ, they also taught them the arts of ecclesiastical poetry, astronomy, and arithmetic. A testimony of which is, that there are still living, at this day some of the scholars, who are as well versed in Greek and Latin tongues as in their own, in which they were born. Nor were there ever happier times since the English came into Britain; for their kings being brave men and good Christians they were a terror to all barbarous nations, and the minds of all men were bent upon the joys of the heavenly kingdom of which they had just heard, and all who desired to be instructed in sacred reading had masters at hand to teach them.

From that time also they began in all the churches of the English to learn sacred music, which till then had been only known in Kent, and, excepting James above mentioned, the first singing master in the churches of the Northumbrians was Eddi, surnamed Stephen, invited

28. Glastonbury Abbey. A view of the abbey church, looking west down the length of the nave. King Ina, about 700, built the great church to the east of the old one. Avalon lay near. Here King Arthur was buried. A leaden cross was inscribed. 'Here lies buried the renowned King Arthur in the Isle of Avalon with Guinevere his second wife.' The sign in the foreground above marks the site where their remains were reinterred in 1278.

from Kent by the most reverend Wilfrid, who was the first of the bishops of the English nation that taught the churches of the English the Catholic mode of life.

Theodore, visiting all parts, ordained bishops in all places, and with their assistance converted such things as he found faulty. . .

Being arrived in the City of Rochester, where the See had been long vacant by the death of Damianius, he ordained a person better skilled in ecclesiastical discipline, and more addicted to simplicity of life than active in worldly affairs. His name was Putta and he was extraordinarily skilful in the Roman style of church music; which he had learned from the disciples of the holy Pope Gregory . . .

A.D. 681. Bishop Wilfrid, when he came into the province (South Saxons), and found so great a misery from famine, taught them to get their food by fishing; for the sea and rivers abounded in fish, but the people had no skill to take them, except eels alone. The bishop's men, having gathered eel-nets everywhere, cast them into the sea, and by the blessing of God took three hundred fishes of several sorts, which, being divided into three parts, they gave a hundred to the poor, a hundred of those of whom they had the nets, and kept a hundred for their own use.

A.D. 731. Such being the peaceable and calm disposition of the times, many of the Northumbrians, as well of the nobility as private persons, laying aside their weapons rather incline to dedicate both themselves and their children to the tonsure and monastic vows, than to studying martial discipline — Bede, *Ecclesiastical History*, IV, ii, translated by J.A. Giles.

King Oswiu in Thanks to God for his Victory Over the Mercians Built a Monastery, and Gives his Daughter in Infancy to the Church, *c.* 654

. . . when, therefore the engagement began, the pagans [Mercians] were put to flight or killed, and thirty royal leaders who had come to his help were nearly all killed; among whom Æthelhere, brother of Anna, king of the East Angles, who reigned after him and was himself the originator of that war, perished after losing his soldiers and auxiliaries. And because the flight took place near the River Winwaed [near Leeds], which owing to the heavy rains had overflowed its channel and all its banks, it happened that the water destroyed far more in flight than the sword in battle.

Then, as he had vowed to the Lord, King Oswiu in thanksgiving for the victory granted to him by God gave his daughter Ælfflaed, who was scarcely a year old, to be dedicated to him in perpetual virginity, granting in addition twelve small estates, on which, since they were set free from concern with earthly military service, a place and means might be provided for monks of zealous devotion to practise celestial military service and to pray for the eternal peace of his nation. He gave six of these small estates in the province of the Deirans, six in that of the Bernicians; and each of the estates was of ten hides, making 120 in all. The aforesaid daughter of King Oswiu who was to be dedicated to God, entered the monastery which is called *Heruteu* [Hartlepool, Durham], that is, 'island of the hart', which Abbess Hilda then presided over; who two years later bought an estate of ten hides in a place which is called *Streoneshealh* [Whitby], and there built a monastery, in which the aforesaid daughter to the king became first a learner of the regular life and afterwards abbess, until, having reached the age of fifty-nine, the blessed virgin entered to the union and marriage with the Heavenly Bridegroom. In this monastery both she herself, and her father, Oswiu, and her mother Eanflaed, and her mother's father, Edwin, and many other noble persons were buried in the church of the holy Apostle Peter.

King Oswiu concluded this war in the district of Leeds in the thirteenth year of his reign, on 15 November, to the great benefit of both nations. For he freed his own nation from the hostile depredations of the pagans and converted that nation of the Mercians and the adjoining provinces to the grace of the faith of Christ, having cut off their heathen chief — Bede's *Ecclesiastical History of the English Nation.* Translation of D. Whitelock partly based on that of J.A. Giles.

Good Carpenter But Bad Monk, 704

I knew a brother myself, would go to God I had not known him, whose name I could mention if it were necessary, and who resided in a noble monastery, but lived himself ignobly. He was frequently reproved by the brethren and elders of the place, and admonished to adopt a more regular life; and though he would not give ear to them, he was long patiently borne with by them, on account of his usefulness in temporal works, for he was an excellent carpenter; he was much addicted to drunkenness, and other pleasures of a lawless life, and more used to stop in his workhouse day and night, than to go to church to sing and pray, and hear the word of life with the brethren. For which reason it happened to him according to the saying, that he who will not willingly and humbly enter the gate of the church, will certainly be damned, and enter the gate of hell whether he will or no. For he falling sick, and being reduced to extremity, called the brethren, and with much lamentation, and like one damned, began to tell them, that he saw hell open, and Satan at the bottom thereof; as also Caiaphas, with the others that slew our Lord, by him delivered up to avenging flames. 'In whose neighbourhood,' said he, 'I see a place of eternal perdition provided for me, miserable wretch.' The brothers, hearing these words, began seriously to exhort him, that he should repent even then whilst he was in the flesh. He answered in despair, 'I have no time now to change my course of life, when I have myself seen my judgment passed.'

Whilst uttering these words, he died without having received the viaticum [the eucharist given to persons in danger of death], and his body was buried in the remotest parts of the monastery, nor did any one dare either to say masses or sing psalms, or even to pray for him. How far has our Lord divided the light from darkness! . . . This happened lately in the province of the Bernicians, and being reported abroad far and near, inclined many to do penance for their sins without delay, which we hope may also be the result of this our narrative – Bede, *Ecclesiastical History,* translated by J.A. Giles.

Part of a Sermon on Hell Attributed to Bede, *c.* 730

. . . it was the Lord's will that Paul should see the punishments of that place. He beheld trees all on fire, and sinners tormented on those trees; and some were hung by their feet, some by their hands, some by their hair, some by the neck, some by the tongue, and some by the arm. And again, he saw a furnace of fire burning with seven flames, and many were punished in it; and there were seven plagues round about this furnace: the first, snow; the second, ice; the third, fire; the fourth, blood; the fifth, serpents; the sixth, lightning; the seventh, stench; and in that furnace itself were the souls of the sinners who repented not in this life. There they are tormented, and every one receiveth according to his works: some weep, some howl, some groan; some burn and desire to have rest, but find it not, because souls can never die. Truly we ought

29. Book of Kells: portrait of St John, about the second half of the
eighth century. 'No surviving manuscript approaches the Book of
Kells either in the elaborate nature of its general scheme of decoration
or in the richness and variety of its details. The creator filled roundels,
borders and isolated rectilinear panels with ribbon and animal interlace
of such incredible delicacy that the unaided eye is quite incapable of
appreciating its microscopic perfection and intricacy' — A.T. Lucas.

to fear that place in which is everlasting dolour, in which is groaning, in which is sadness without joy, in which are abundance of tears on account of the tortures of souls; in which a fiery wheel is turned a thousand times every day by an evil angel, and at each turn a thousand souls are burnt upon it. After this he beheld a horrible river, in which were many diabolic beasts, like fishes in the midst of the sea, which devour the souls of sinners; and over that river there is a bridge, across which righteous souls pass without dread, while the souls of sinners suffer each according to its merits . . . – from Rev. J.M. Neale, *Medieval Preachers and Medieval Preaching.*

St Cuthbert Forbade Women to Enter Certain Cemeteries, 878

This custom is so diligently observed, even unto the present day, that it is unlawful for women to set foot even within the cemeteries of those churches in which his body obtained a temporary resting-place, unless, indeed, compelled to do so by the approach of an enemy or the dread of fire.

There have been women, however, who in their boldness have ventured to infringe these decrees; but the punishment which has speedily overtaken them, gave proof of the magnitude of their crime. One of these, named Sungeova, the wife of the son of Bevo, who was named Gamel, as she was one night returning home from an entertainment, was continually complaining to her husband that there was no clean piece of road to be found, in consequence of the deep puddles with which it was everywhere studded. So at last they determined that they would go through the churchyard (that is, of Durham), and that they would afterwards make an atonement for this sin by almsgiving. As they were going on together, she was seized with some kind of indefinite horror, and cried out that she was gradually losing her senses. Her husband chid her, and urged her to come on, and not to be afraid; but as soon as she set foot outside the hedge which surrounds the cemetery of the church, she immediately fell down; and being carried home, she that very night ended her life.

. . . A certain rich man – who afterwards resided amongst us in this church, wearing the dress of a monk – had a wife; and she, having heard many persons talk of the beauty of the ornaments of the church was inflamed, woman-like, with the desire of seeing these novelties.

Unable to bridle her impetuous desires, for the power of her husband elevated her above her neighbours, she walked through the cemetery of the church — Simeon of Durham, translated by Rev. J. Stevenson in *The Church Historians of England.*

Monastic Life Before St Dunstan, *c*. 890

I do not consider it profitable to pass over in this place his [Alfred's] vow and most well-thought-out scheme, which he was never able to put aside by any means either in prosperity or adversity. For when in his usual manner he was meditating on the needs of his soul, among other good acts in which he was actively engaged by day and night, he ordered the foundation of two monasteries; one for monks in the place called Athelney, which is surrounded in all sides by very great swampy and impassable marshes, so that no one can approach it by any means except in punts, or by a bridge which has been made with laborious skill between two fortresses. At the western end of this bridge a very strong fort has been placed of most beautiful workmanship by the king's command. In this monastery he collected monks of various races from every quarter, and set them therein.

For at first he had no noble or freeman of his own nation who would of his own accord enter the monastic life — apart from children, who by reason of their tender age could not yet choose good or refuse evil — for indeed for many years past the desire for the monastic life had been utterly lacking in all that people, and also in many other nations, although there still remain many monasteries founded in that land, but none properly observing the rule of this way of life, I know not why; whether on account of the onslaughts of foreigners, who very often invaded by land or sea, or on account of the nation's too great abundance of riches of every kind, which I am much more inclined to think the reason for that contempt of the monastic life. For this reason he sought to gather together monks of different race in the monastery.

First, he appointed John, priest and monk, by race an Old Saxon, as abbot, and then some priests and deacons from across the sea. But when he still had not with these the number he wanted, he also procured many of that same Gallic race, some of whom, being children, he ordered to be educated in that same monastery, and to be raised to the monastic order at a later time. In that monastery I also saw one

30. Cross of Patrick and Columba, Kells, Co. Meath, Ireland. Early ninth century.

of pagan race, brought up there and wearing the monastic habit, quite a young man, and not the lowest among them — Asser, *Life of King Alfred,* translated by L.C. Jane.

Homily on the Feast of St John the Baptist, Ninth Century

In worshyp of Saint Johan the people waked [kept holiday] at home, and made three maner of fyres: one was clene bones, and noo woode, and that is called a Bone Fyre, for people to sit and wake thereby; another is clene woode, and no bones, and that is called a Wode Fyre, for people to sit and wake thereby; the thirde is made of wode and bones, and it is callyd Saynt Johannys fyre. The first fyre, as a great clerke Johan Belleth telleth he was in a certegne countrey, so in the countrey there was soo greate hete the which causid that dragons to go togyther in tokenynge that Johan dyed in brennynge love and charyté to God and man, and they that dye in charyté shall have parte of all good prayers, and they that do not, shall never be saved. Then as these dragons flewe in th'ayre they shed down to that water froth of ther kynde, and so envenymed the waters, and caused moche people for to take theyr deth thereby, and many dyverse skyenesse. Wyse clerkes knoweth well that dragons hate nothyng more than the stenche of brennynge bones, and therefore they gaderyd as many as they mighte fynde, and brent them; and so with the stenche thereof they drove away the dragons, and so they were brought out of greete dysease. The second fyre was made of woode, for that wyl brenne lyght, and wyll be seen farre. For it is the chefe of fyre to be seen farre, and betokenneth that Saynt Johan was a lanterne of lyght to the people. Also the people mad blases of fyre, for that they shulde be seene farre, and specyally in the nyght, in tokens of St. Johan's having been seen from far in the spirit by Jeremiah. The third fyre of bones betokenneth Johan's martyrdome, for hys bones were brente [burnt by Julian the Apostle] — Homily on the Feast of St John the Baptist, appearing in a discussion of the customs of Midsummer Eve, J. Brand, *Observations on the Popular Antiquities of Great Britain.*

St Dunstan, Artist and Craftsman, 924-988

Among his sacred studies of literature he also diligently cultivated the art of writing that he might be sufficient in all things; and the art of harp-playing, and skill in painting likewise; and, so to speak, he excelled as a keen investigator of all useful things. On this account a certain noble woman called Aethelwynn called him to her on one occasion with a friendly request to design her a stole for the divine service with divers figures, which she could afterwards diversify and adorn with gold and gems. When he came to her for this work, he usually brought with him his *cythera*, which in the native language we call 'harp', that he might at times delight himself and the hearts of his listeners in it. Then one day after dinner, when he and the aforesaid woman returned with her workwomen to the said work, it happened by a marvellous event that this same harp of the blessed champion, hanging on the wall of the chamber, rang out a melody of jubilation of its own accord, without anyone touching it, with a clear sound in the hearing of all. For it rang out and played the melody of this anthem, and continued chanting the melody right through to the end: 'Let the souls of the saints who followed the steps of Christ rejoice in the heavens; and because they shed their blood for his love, they shall reign with Christ for ever.' And when they heard it, he and the aforesaid woman and all her workwomen were terrified, and completely forgetting the work in their hands, gazed at one another in astonishment, marvelling greatly what new warning that miraculous act might prefigure — Life of St Dunstan, edited by W. Stubbs, *Memorials of St Dunstan,* translated by Dorothy Whitelock, *English Historical Documents*, Vol. I. This, the oldest life, is dedicated to Aelfric, Archbishop of Canterbury, 995-1005.

Hearth-Penny, *c.* 950

And let every hearth-penny be rendered by St. Peter's massday: and he who shall not have paid it by that term, let him be led to Rome, and in addition thereto pay 30 pence, and bring then a certificate thence, that he has there rendered so much; and when he comes home, pay to the king a hundred and twenty shillings. And if again he will not pay it, let him be led again to Rome, and with another such 'bot' [indemnification]; and when he comes home, pay to the king two hundred shillings. At the third time, if he then yet will not, let him forfeit all he owns — Laws of King Edgar (956-75), I, 4, B. Thorpe, *Ancient Laws and Institutes of England.*

Of Parish Priests, *c.* 960

... And we enjoin them, that they, at every synod, have, every year, books and garments for divine ministry, and ink and vellum for their ordinances; and provision for three days.

And we enjoin, that every priest at the synod have his clerk, and an orderly man for servant, and no ignorant person who loves folly; but let all go with decorum, and with fear of God Almighty . . . .

And we enjoin, that no priest receive another's scholar, without leave of him who he previously followed.

And we enjoin, that every priest, in addition to lore, diligently learn a handicraft.

And we enjoin, that no learned priest put to shame the half learned, but improve him, if he know better.

And we enjoin, that no high born priest despise the lower born; because if it be rightly considered, then are all men of one birth.

And we enjoin, that every priest provide for himself lawfully, and let no one be a monger unlawfully, nor a covetous merchant.

And we enjoin, that every priest grant baptism as soon as it is demanded; and everywhere, in his shrift-district, command, that every child be baptized within 37 days; and that no one be too long unconfirmed.

And we enjoin, that every priest zealously promote Christianity, and totally extinguish every heathenism; and forbid well-worshippings, and necromancies, and divinations, and enchantments, and man-worshippings, and the vain practices which are carried on with various spells, and with 'frith-splots' [sacred spots], and with elders, and also with various trees, and with stones, and with many various delusions, with which men do much of what they should not — Canons Enacted under King Edgar (956-75), B. Thorpe, *Ancient Laws and Institutes of England.*

31. Frontispiece of the *Liber Vitae* of New Minster, Winchester, *c.* 1016-20. Top: St Peter beckons the saved to Heaven. Centre: The devil and St Peter struggle over one soul. Bottom: an angel locks the door of Hell.

How to Gain Penance, *c*. 960

Thus may a powerful man, and rich in friends, with the support of his friends, greatly lighten his penance . . . Let him then lay aside his weapons, and vain ornaments, and take a staff in his hand, and go barefoot zealously, and put on his body woollen or haircloth, and not come into a bed, but lie on a pallet, and so do, that in three days the series of 7 years be dispensed with thus: let him proceed with aid; and first let him take to him 12 men, and let them fast 3 days on bread, and on green herbs, and on water; and get, in addition thereto, in whatever manner he can, seven times 120 men, who shall also fast for him 3 days; then will be fasted as many fasts as there are days in 7 years.

When a man fasts, then let the dishes that would have been eaten be all distributed to God's poor; and the three days that a man fasts, let him abandon every worldly occupation, and by day and by night, the oftenest that he can, let him remain in church, and with almslight earnestly watch there, and cry to God, and implore forgiveness, with groaning spirit, and kneel frequently on the sign of the cross; sometimes up, sometimes down, extend himself; and let the powerful man try earnestly to shed tears from his eyes, and bewail his sins; and let a man then feed those three days as many of God's poor as he possibly can; and on the fourth day, bathe them all, and shelter them, and distribute money; and let the penitent himself employ himself in washing their feet, and let as many masses be said for him on that day as can possibly be obtained, and at the last, let absolution be given — Canons enacted under King Edgar (956-75), B. Thorpe, *Ancient Laws and Institutes of England.*

Service for the Dead, *c*. 970

When the brother has departed his life, his body shall be washed by those appointed to do so: when washed it is clothed in clean garments namely, in shirt, cowl, stockings and shoes, no matter what his rank. But if he is a priest a stole may be placed about him over his cowl, if such be the rule. The body shall then be borne into the church with the chanting of psalms and the tolling of bells. And if the brother died before dawn, in the night or after the dark hours, in the early morning, let him be buried before the brethren have their meal, when the Masses have been celebrated, provided that those things necessary for a burial can be prepared: otherwise let the brethren be appointed by turns to chant psalms unceasingly by the body throughout the day and the following night until early morning when it shall be committed to the earth.

When all things proper to the Burial Office have been completed, let the brethren straightway begin the seven Penitential psalms and, returning to the church let them prostrate before the holy altar, finish those psalms for the dead brother. Thenceforward for seven successive days the Office of the Dead shall be said in full, and all shall make the offering at the Morrow Mass; moreover, after each of the regular hours they shall sing, prostrate, one of the Penitential psalms followed by a prayer. Thenceforth until the thirtieth day the Office of the Dead shall be said daily with three lessons as usual, one choir at a time making the offering at Mass. But on the thirteenth day the Office of the Dead shall again be said in full. During these thirty days each priest shall say a special Mass daily for the dead brother, in the secret places of the oratory; and with all devotion each deacon shall chant the entire Psalter and each subdeacon fifty psalms; and if on account of his work he cannot do this on one day he shall do so on another – *Regularis Concordia Anglicae Nationis Monachorum Sanctimonialum,* translated by Dom Thomas Symons.

Morning Ritual, *c.* 970

When the bell is rung the brethren shall go and put on their day shoes: none but the ministers should presume to do this before the bell is heard. Nor fail to do so then without permission, lest the merit of obedience be sadly dimmed by his rashness and presumption. Next the entire *schola* [choir school] with their master and the abbot shall wash their faces as is customary, intent on the psalms as they do so. As for the seniors, let each one separately, according as God suggests to his heart by His divine inspiration, silently and with the whole bent of his mind apply himself to his duty, sanctifying his acts of obedience, as he should everything, with holy prayers, chanting the canonical hours, or the seven Penitential psalms or any other spiritual prayer apt for driving away the temptation of the devil; and so, having washed, let them proceed to the church. As the children enter the church the sacrist shall ring the first bell; and when they have said the *Trina oratio* [a prayer in honour of the Trinity] in the same way as the seniors have done, all shall take their places and the bell shall be rung for them to begin Tierce — *Regularis Concordia Anglicae Nationis Monachorum Sanctimonialium*, translated by Dom Thomas Symons.

An Old English Account of King Edgar's Establishment of Monasteries, *c.* 970

... we also instruct abbesses to be deeply loyal and to serve the precepts of the holy rule with all their hearts, and to enjoin the commands of God Almighty so that none of them shall presume senselessly to give God's estates either to their kinsman or to secular great persons, neither for money nor for flattery. Let them consider that they are set as shepherds on God's behalf, and not as robbers. If any one of them, led astray by the temptation of the devil, be convicted of crime against the Church or the state, let neither king nor secular lord [owner of private jurisdiction, who would benefit by fines] be glad of it, as if the way were cleared and a reason given for him to rob God, who owns those possessions, and who never committed any crime; nor indeed let the heavenly king who created him be entitled to the same rights as he is himself. If any of the king's reeves is convicted of crime against God or man, what man is so foolish or senseless as to deprive the king of his property because his reeve is convicted? Therefore in the same way let whatever among the possessions of the churches is given to the eternal Christ stand for ever. If anyone is so presumptuous that he perverts this, he shall be miserably tormented in eternal torments. May it not come to pass that any of my successors shall deserve such wretchedness! — probably written by Aethelwold, Bishop of Winchester, translated by O. Cockayne, *Leechdoms, Wortcunning and Starcraft of Early England.*

The Rule of St Benedict Now in English, *c.* 975

With earnest scrutiny he [Edgar] began to investigate and enquire about the precepts of the holy Rule, and wished to know the teaching of that same Rule, by which is laid down the practice of a right life and honourable vocation, and the regulations which attract men to holy virtues. He wished also to know from the Rule the wise disposition which is prudently appointed concerning the ordering of unfamiliar matters. Out of a wish for this knowledge he commanded this Rule to be translated from the Latin into the English language.

Although keen-witted scholars do not require this English translation, it is nevertheless necessary for unlearned laymen who for fear of hell-torment and for the love of Christ abandon this wretched life and turn to their Lord and choose the holy service of this Rule; lest any unconverted layman should in ignorance and stupidity break the precepts of the Rule and employ the excuse that he erred on that day because he knew no better. I [Aethelwold] therefore considered this translation a very sensible thing. It certainly does not matter by what language a man is acquitted and drawn to the true faith, as long only as he come to God. Therefore let the unlearned natives have the knowledge of this holy rule by the exposition of their own language, that they may the more zealously serve God and have no excuse that they were driven by ignorance to err — Aethelwold, King Edgar's Establishment of Monasteries, *English Historical Documents,* Vol. I.

Easter Service

Angel voice about Christ's Resurrection:

'Whom do ye seek in the sepulchre, O folk of Christ?' Answer of the holy women (the three Marys):

'Jesus of Nazareth the crucified, O folk of Heaven. Consolation of the angel voice':

'He is not here, He has risen as he foretold. Go and tell forth the news for He is risen.'

Song of the holy women to all the clergy:

'Alleluia, the Lord is risen today, the strong lion is risen, Christ, the son of God. Thanks be to God, raise the joyful cry! Come and see the place where the Lord was laid, alleluia, alleluia.'

Again let the angel speak:

'Hasten, hasten and tell the disciples, for the Lord is risen, alleluia, alleluia.'

The women sing with one voice in gladness:

'The Lord is risen from the sepulchre, He who hung upon the wood for us, alleluia.'

Translated from Winchester Trope, 978-80,
Karl Young, *The Drama of the Mediaeval Church.*

Of Holy Days, Tenth Century

And we enjoin, that on feast-days heathen songs and devil's games be abstained from.

And we enjoin, that Sunday trading, and folk-moots, be abstained from.

And we enjoin, that unbecoming garments, and foolish discourses, and ignominious shavings be abstained from . . .

And we enjoin, that on feast-days, and lawful fast-days, there be no strife, among men, to any excess.

And we enjoin, that on feast-days and fast-days, oaths and ordeals be foregone . . .

And we enjoin, that every one, at the church wakes, be very sober, and earnestly pray, and suffer there be no drinking, nor any vanity.

Canons enacted under King Edgar (956-75), B. Thorpe,
Ancient Laws and Institutes of England.

The Passing of a Viking, Heroic Age Pagan King

As for Scyld [Danish Chieftain], he departed, at the destined hour, full of exploit, to go into the Master's keeping. They then carried him forth to the shore of the sea, his faithful comrades, as he himself had requested, while he with his words held sway as lord of the Scyldings; dear chief of the land, he had long tenure of power.

There at the landing-place stood the ship with ringed prow, glistening afresh, and outward bound; convoy for a prince. Down laid they there the beloved chief, dispenser of jewels, on the lap of the ship, the illustrious dead by the mast.

There was store of precious things, ornaments from remote ports, brought together; never heard I of craft comelier fitted with slaughter weapons and campaigning harness, with swords and breast-mail. In his keeping lay a multitude of treasures, which were to pass with him far away into the watery realm.

Not at all with less gifts, less stately opulence, did they outfit him, than those had done, who at the first had sent him forth, lone over the wave, when he was an infant. Furthermore, they set up by him a gold wrought banner, high over his head. They let the flood bear him, gave him over to the ocean; sad was their soul, mourning their mood. Who received that burthen, men, heads of Halls, heroes under heaven cannot for certain tell — *The Deeds of Beowulf*, Prologue, translated by J. Earle.

From 'Sermon of the Wolf to the English', 1014

Lupus, 'the Wolf', was the literary name used by Wulfstan, bishop of London 996 to 1002, archbishop of York 1002 to 1023. He wrote homilies and composed a good deal of the legislation of the reigns of Ethelred and Cnut.

The sermon of the Wolf to the English when the Danes persecuted them most, which was in the Year 1014 from the incarnation of our Lord Jesus Christ.

Alas for the misery, and alas for the public shame which the English now have, all through God's anger. Often two sea-men, or maybe three, drive the droves of Christian men from sea to sea, out through this people, huddled together, as a public shame to us all, if we could seriously and rightly feel any shame. But all the insult which we often suffer we repay with honouring those who insult us; we pay them continually and they humiliate us daily; they ravage and they burn, plunder and rob and carry on board; and lo, what else is there in all these events except God's anger clear and visible over this people?

It is no wonder that things go wrong with us, for we know full well that now for many years men have too often not cared what they did by word or deed; but this people, as it may seem, has become very corrupt through manifold sins and many misdeeds; through murders and crimes, through avarice and through greed, through theft and robbery, through the selling of men and through heathen vices, through betrayals and frauds, through breaches of law and through deceit, through attacks on kinsmen and through slayings, through injury of men in holy orders and through adultery, through incest and through various fornications. And also, far and wide, as we said before, more than should be are lost and perjured through the breaking of oaths and pledges and through various falsehoods; and failure to observe fasts and festivals widely occurs again and again.

And also there are here in the country degenerate apostates [God's adversaries] and fierce persecutors of the Church and cruel tyrants all too many, and widespread scorners of divine laws and Christian virtues, and foolish deriders everywhere among the people, most often of those things which God's messengers command, and especially of those things which always belong to God's law by rights. And therefore things have now come far and wide to that full evil pass that men are more ashamed now of good deeds than of misdeeds, for too often good deeds are reviled with derision and godfearing people are blamed all too greatly, and especially are those reproached and all too often treated with contempt who love right and possess the fear of God in any extent.

And because people behave thus, blaming all that they should praise, and loathing too much what they should love, they bring all too many to evil intentions and wicked acts, so that they are not ashamed, although they sin greatly and commit wrongs even against God himself, but because of idle calumny they are ashamed to atone for their misdeeds as the books teach [penitentials used in the Anglo-Saxon Church], like those fools who because of their pride will not protect themselves from injury until they cannot, although they much wish it — Wulfstan, archbishop of York, Sermon to the English, *English Historical Documents,* Vol. I.

Some Priests Behave Badly, *c.* 1020

Let him make 'bot' [amends] for it:
if a priest despise or insult another with word or deed;
if a priest fight with another;
if a priest be aiding to another in wrong;
if a priest refuse another lawful succour;
if a priest leave another unwarned of that which he knows will harm him;
if a priest neglect the shaving of beard or of locks;
if a priest, at the appointed time, do not ring the hours, or sing the hours;
if a priest come with weapons into a church;

if a priest misorder the annual services of the church, by day or by
    night;
if a priest misconduct an ordeal;
if a priest enwrap his tonsure;
if a priest love drunkenness, or become a gleeman or an 'ale-
    scop' . . .
If a priest forsake a woman and take another, let him
    be excommunicated.

                     Law of the Northumbrian Priests, B. Thorpe,
                          Ancient Laws and Institutes of England.

11 Law and Crime

From the Laws of Hlothhere and Eadric,
Kings of Kent, 673-685

11.   If anyone in another's house calls a man a perjurer, or shamefully accosts him with insulting words, he is to pay a shilling to him who owns the house, and six shillings to him to whom he spoke that word, and to pay 12 shillings to the king.

12.   If anyone removes a cup from another where men are drinking, without provocation, he shall according to ancient law pay a shilling to him who owns the house, and six shillings to him whose cup was removed, and 12 shillings to the king.

13.   If anyone draws a weapon where men are drinking, and yet no injury is done there, [he is to pay] a shilling to him who owns the house and 12 shillings to the king.

14.   If the house is stained by bloodshed, he is to pay to the man [the owner of the house] the price for breach of his protection, and 50 shillings to the king.

15.   If anyone harbours a stranger, a trader or any other man who has come across the frontier, for three nights in his own home, and then supplies him with his food, and he then does any injury to any man, the host is to bring the other to justice or to discharge the obligations for him.

16.   If a man of Kent buys property in London, he is to have then two or three honest *ceorls*, or the king's town-reeve, as witness.

16. 1.   If then it is attached in the possession of the man in Kent, he is to vouch to warranty the man who sold it to him, at the king's hall in that town, if he knows him and can produce him at that vouching to warranty.

16. 2. If he cannot do that, he is then to declare at the altar with one of his witnesses or with the king's town-reeve, that he bought that property openly by a public transaction [or 'with goods known to be his'] in the town, and he is then to be given back his price.

16. 3. If, then, he cannot declare that with proper exculpation, he is to relinquish it, and the owner is to succeed to it — the Code survives in the *Textus Roffensis*, edited by F. Liebermann, translated by F.L. Attenborough and B. Thorpe.

From the Laws of Ine, King of Wessex, Recorded between 688 and 694

They survived because King Alfred appended a copy of them to his own code of laws.

The Organisation of Colonies

[When a man] intends to depart, he who has 20 hides [varied from 60 to 120 acres] shall show 12 hides cultivated; he who has 10 hides shall show 6 cultivated, he who has 3 shall show 1½.

The laws also declare that
if a nobleman depart, he may take with him his reeve, his smith, and his children's tutor.

Unauthorised emigration was forbidden
If a man departs from his lord without permission and steals away into another shire, and is discovered, he shall return to where he was, and pay his lord 60 shillings.

Other laws concern new homes of the colonists. Those related to a ceorl's worth [a self-contained individual farm] applied to all Wessex. They stated that

a *ceorl's worth* shall be fenced in summer and in winter. If not, and a neighbour's beast strays through the gap he has left, he shall have no claim on the beast; he shall chase it out and accept the damage.

If *ceorls* have a grass enclosure, or other apportioned land to fence, and some have fenced their part and some have not, and cattle get in and eat their common arable or grass, those responsible for the gap shall offer compensation for the damage done to the others, who have enclosed their part. They shall demand from the owners of the cattle whatever reparation is proper.

But if a beast breaks through the *hegas* [hedge] and wanders within, since its owner cannot or will not control it, he who finds it on his arable shall take it and kill it. The owner shall have its hide and flesh, and accept the loss of the rest — *English Historical Documents*, Vol. I.

Punishments for Pagans and Others Who Turn from the Church of God, *c.* 690

1. The Apostle says: 'No one who serves idols will possess the kingdom of God.' If anyone makes minor sacrifices to demons he will do penance for 1 year; and 10 years for major sacrifices.
2. If any one eats or drinks in ignorance by a heathen shrine he is to promise never to do so again and to do 40 days penance on bread and water. If he does it deliberately, that is to say after a priest has declared that it is sacrilege and the table of demons he shall do penance on bread and water for thrice 40 days. But if he did it in honour of the demons and to glorify the idol, he is to do penance for 3 years.
3. If anyone sacrifices to demons for a second or a third time he incurs 3 years penance; then 2 years without any offering of communion. In the third five years, at the end of a five year period, he is capable of perfection.
4. If anyone eat what has been sacrificed to idols and was under no compulsion, he is to fast 12 weeks on bread and water; if it was done of necessity he is to fast 6 weeks.
5. If any keep feasts in the abominable places of the heathen, taking and eating their food there, they should be subject to penance for 2 years, and be offered on probation for full two years, and after that be accepted to perfection; when offered test the spirit and discuss the life of each individual.
6. If any do sacrilege, that is summon diviners who practise divination by birds, or does any divination with evil intent, let him do penance for 3 years, and for one of these on bread and water.
7. Christians may not leave the Church of God and go to divination, or name angels or make covins which are known to be forbidden. If any be found serving this occult idolatry, in that he abandons our Lord Jesus Christ, the son of God, and gave himself to idolatry . . .
8. It is unlawful for clerks or laymen, to be sorcerers or inchanters, or

to make amulets which are proved to be fetters for their souls; those who act thus we command to be driven from the Church.

32. *The Fates of Men* describes how 'One shall swing on the broad gallows, hang in death, until the body, the frame, is bloodily destroyed.'

9. If anyone destroy a person by black magic he is to do penance for 7 years, 3 of these on bread and water.
10. If any use love potions and hurt nobody, if he is a layman he is to do penance for half a year; if he is a clerk, 1 year on bread and water; if he is a subdeacon, he is to do penance for 2 years, 1 year on bread and water; if he is a deacon, 4, 2 on bread and water; if he is priest, 5 years, 3 on bread and water. But if thereby any one deceive a woman of her bringing forth, then he is to do further 3 years penance on bread and water, lest he be accused of homicide.
11. If anyone seeks diviners whom they call prophets, or does any divinations, in that this too is diabolical, let him do penance 5 years, 3 of these on bread and water.
12. If anyone take lots, which they call contrary to the principles of the Saints, or have any lots whatsoever, or take lots with evil intent, or make divination, let him do penance 3 years, 1 on bread and water.

13. If any woman do divinations or diabolical incantations, let her do penance 1 year, or thrice 40 days or 40 days, according to the enormity of the crime of the penitent.
14. If any woman place her son or daughter on the roof for the sake of a cure or in an oven, let her do penance 7 years.
15. If any burn grain where a man has died for the sake of the living or of the house, let him do penance 5 years on bread and water.
16. If any for the health of his little son should pass through a fissure in the ground and should close it after himself with thorns, let him do penance 40 days on bread and water.
17. If any seek out divinations and pursue them in the manner of the heathen, or introduce such men into their houses, for the sake of finding something out by evil arts or to make an expiation, let them be cast out if they be of the clergy; but if they are secular let them after confession be subjected to 5 years of penance, according to the rules ordained of old.
18. If any make or perform a vow at trees, or springs, or stones, or boundaries, or anywhere at all except in the house of God, let him do penance for 3 years on bread and water. This is sacrilege or diabolical. If any eat or drink there let him do penance for 1 year on bread and water.
19. If any go at the New Year as a young stag or cow, that is, if he share the habit of wild beasts and is clad in the skins of cattle and puts on the heads of beasts, any such who thus transform themselves into the likenesses of beasts are to do 3 years penance.
20. If any one is an astrologer [*mathematicus*], that is one who changes the mind of a man by the invocation of devils, he is to do 5 years penance, 1 on bread and water.
21. If anyone is a sender of storm, that is to say a sorcerer, he is to do penance 7 years, 3 on bread and water.
22. If anyone makes amulets, which is detestable, he should do 3 years penance, 1 on bread and water.
23. Anyone who makes a habit of auguries and divinations is to do penance 5 years.
24. Any who observe soothsayers, or inchanters, and devilish amulets and dreams and herbs, or who keep holy the fifth day in honour of Jove [Jeudi; or of Thor: Thursday], or New Year's Day, as do the heathen, is to do penance 5 years if a clerk and 3 years if a layman.
25. Those who take care when the moon is eclipsed to practise as they trust by their cries and witchcrafts to defend her in sacriligious fashion are to do penance 5 years.

26. Those who fast in honour of the moon to bring about healing are
to do penance 1 year — from B. Thorpe, *Ancient Laws and Institutes of England.*

Punishments for Drunkenness and for Causing it, *c.* 690

If a bishop, priest or deacon or anyone in holy orders has a fault in the
habit of drunkenness, he is to stop or to be deposed. If a priest or deacon vomits through drunkenness he is to do penance for 40 days with
bread and water; a subdeacon 30 days; a clerk 20; a layman 15. If a
monk vomits through drunkenness he is to do penance 30 days. If
through drunkenness or greed a bishop should vomit up the eucharist
he is to do penance for 90 days; a priest for 70; a deacon and a monk
for 60; a clerk 40; a layman 30. If the cause is illness each should do 7
days; some a psalter, some the psalter twice. If he casts forth the sacri-
fice into the fire or into a river, he should sing 100 psalms. If dogs
devour it he should do penance for 100 days if it is with his knowledge;
otherwise 40 days. If a faithful layman makes another drunk through
wickedness, let him do penance 40 days. If any priest, deacon, monk,
subdeacon, clerk or layman vomits through illness he is blameless. If
anyone has been abstinent for a long time and was not accustomed to
drink and eat much, or if through festivity at Christmas or at Easter or
for the commemoration of any of the Saints he has been sick, if on
such an occasion he has not taken more than was ordained by his
elders, he is guiltless. If priests become drunk through ignorance they
are to do penance on bread and water for 7 days. If it is through negli-
gence, 15 days. If through wantonness, they should do penance 40
days; deacons and monks 4 weeks; subdeacons 3; clerks 2; and laymen
1 week. If anyone compels a man to get drunk through kindness he is
to do penance 20 days. If he did it for spite he is to be adjudged as a
homicide. If any priest, or deacon, or clerk, drinks so much that he
cannot sing the psalms but stumbles in his speech, let him do penance
on bread and water for 12 days and purge his sin. If anybody feels an
excessive swelling of his belly and pain through over-eating, that is to
say to the point of vomiting without being ill, let him do penance for 7
days with bread and water. If any become drunk on wine or ale against
the command of the Lord Saviour and His Apostles [drunkenness is
defined as a change of mood, lack of control over the tongue, rolling
eyes, giddiness of head, swelling of belly and consequent ache] , a lay-

man should do penance with bread for 1 week; a clerk for 2 weeks; a subdeacon for 15 days; a deacon and a monk for 3 weeks; a priest for 4; and a bishop for 5. If any clerk through gluttony takes food before the canonical hour and without the necessity of illness he is to have no dinner and to do penance for 2 days on bread and water — Penitential of Archbishop Theodore (d. 690), B. Thorpe, *Ancient Laws and Institutes of England.*

Of Usury: No Unjust Interest, *c.* 735

It is forbidden to all believers to lend money or goods for any unjust interest. That is to say no demand is to be made for a return of more than what was originally lent; but anyone who makes a loan of money or goods to another must do it for love and out of necessity, just as he would wish that it were done to himself. If any one do this out of wicked avarice, the sacred books prescribe for him a fast of 3 years, 1 year with bread and water and 2 according as his confessor prescribes for him . . .

If a bishop or an abbot or a priest or any minister of God whatsoever makes a loan of money for interest which is unjust and does not remember that which the Saviour says through the Psalmist David that those enjoy His kingdom who do not lend their money for usury [*Psalm* 15.5] ; if any violate this law he is not worthy to receive the Eucharist, before he has amended, as is written above, that is to say through a fast of 3 years — Penitential of Archbishop Ecgbert, 735-66, B. Thorpe, *Ancient Laws and Institutes of England.*

Punishments for Sorcery, Soothsaying and Making Use of Potions, *c.*750

If any stick a needle in any man let him fast 3 years, 1 year with bread and water, and for 2 years with bread and water on 3 days in the week. And if a man die of the prick then let him fast 7 years, as is above written.

And if any make use of potions, for the sake of the love of anyone, and give anything in the food or the drink or by inchantments of any sort that their love may be thereby increased; if a layman do this, let him fast for half a year on Wednesdays and Fridays on bread and water and let him eat his food on other days, excepting only meat. If he is a clerk let him fast 1 year, on bread and water on 2 days in the week, and on the other days let him abstain from meat. If he is a deacon, let him fast 3 years, on bread and water on two days each week and let him abstain from meat on the other days. If he is a priest let him fast 5 years, 1 on bread and water and for 4 with bread and water on Fridays, and on the other days let him abstain from meat.

If any exercise divinations and soothsayings or keep vigils at any spring or at any other creature, except at the church of God, let him fast for 3 years, 1 on bread and water and 2 on bread and water on Wednesdays and Fridays, and on the other days let him have his food except meat only.

A woman deserves the same if she cure her child by any sorcery or if she draw it over the ground to the cross roads — Penitential of Archbishop Ecgbert (735-66), B. Thorpe, *Ancient Laws and Institutes of England.*

Some Penalties for Severe Wounds, *c.* 890

Laws of King Alfred

If a man's arm with the hand, be entirely cut off before the elbow, let 'bōt' [reparation] be made for it LXXX shillings.

If a man break another's rib within the whole skin, let X shillings be paid as 'bōt'; if the skin be broken, and bone be taken out let XV shillings be paid as 'bōt'.

Laws of King Aethelbirht

If a thumb be struck off, XX shillings. If a thumb nail be torn off let 'bōt' be made with III shillings. If the shooting [fore] finger be struck off let 'bōt' be made with VIII shillings. If the middle finger be struck off let 'bōt' be made with IV shillings. If the gold [ring] finger be struck off, let 'bōt' be made with VI shillings. If the little finger be struck off, let 'bōt' be made with XI shillings.

For every nail a shilling.

If a foot be cut off let L shillings be paid.

If a great toe be cut off let X shillings be paid.

For each of the other toes let one half be paid, like as is stated for the fingers — from B. Thorpe, *Ancient Laws and Institutes.*

Trial by Ordeal, 924-939

23. If anyone pledges [to undergo] the ordeal, he is then to come three days before to the priest whose duty it is to consecrate it, and live off bread and water and salt and vegetables until he shall go to it, and be present at mass on each of those three days, and make his offering and go to communion on the day on which he shall go to the ordeal, and swear then the oath that he is guiltless of that charge according to the common law, before he goes to the ordeal.

23.1. And if it is [the ordeal of] water, he is to sink one and a half ells on the rope; if it is the ordeal of iron, it is to be three days before the hand is unbound — Laws of Aethelstan at Grately, *English Historical Documents*, Vol. I.

The Law of Sanctuary, Tenth Century

5. Also we determine this sanctuary for every church which a bishop has consecrated: if a man exposed to a vendetta reaches it running or riding, no one is to drag him out for seven days, if he can live in spite of hunger, unless he himself fights [his way] out. If then anyone does so, he is liable to [pay for breach of] the king's protection and of the church's sanctuary — more, if he seizes more from there.

5.1. If the community have more need of their church, he is to be kept in another building, and it is to have no more doors than the church.

5.2. The head of that church is to take care that no one gives him food during that period.

5.3. If he himself will hand out his weapons to his foes, they are to keep him for 30 days, and send notice about him to his kinsmen.

5.4. Further sanctuary of the church: if any man has recourse to the church on account of any crime which has not been discovered, and there confesses himself in God's name, it is to be half remitted.

5.5. Whoever steals on Sunday or at Christmas or Easter or on the Holy Thursday in Rogation days; each of those we wish to be compensated doubly, as in the Lenten fast — Laws of Alfred, *English Historical Documents*, Vol. I.

Coinage, *c.* 930

We ordain ... that there be one money over all the king's dominion, and that no man mint except within port. And if the moneyer [maker of coin] be guilty, let the hand be struck off with which he wrought that offence, and be set up on the money-smithy; but if it be an accusation, and he is willing to clear himself; then let him go to the hot-iron, and clear the hand therewith with which he is charged that fraud to have wrought. And if at the ordeal he should be guilty, let the like be done as is here before ordained.

    In Canterbury 7 moneyers — 4 the king's and 2 the bishop's and 1 the abbot's.
    At Rochester 3 — 2 the king's and 1 the bishop's.
    At London 8.
    At Winchester 6.
    At Lewes 2.
    At Hastings 1.
    Another at Chichester.
    At Hampton 2.
    At Wareham 2.
    At Exeter 2.
    At Shaftesbury 2.
    Else, at the other burgs 1 — The Laws of King Aethelstan, I, 14, B. Thorpe, *Ancient Laws and Institutes of England.*

Trial by Ordeal, Hot Iron and Water, *c.* 930

And concerning the ordeal we enjoin by the command of God, and of the archbishop, and of all the bishops; that no man come within the church after the fire is borne in with which the ordeal shall be heated, except the mass-priest, and him who shall go thereto. Let there be measured nine feet from the stake to the mark, by the man's feet who goes thereto. But if it be water, let it be heated till it low to boiling. And be the kettle of iron or of brass or of lead or of clay. And if it be a single accusation, let the hand dive after the stone up to the wrist; and if it be threefold, up to the elbow.
    And when the ordeal is ready, then let two men go in of either side;

and be they agreed that it is so hot as we before have said. And let go in an equal number of men of either side and stand on both sides of the ordeal, along the church; and let these all be fasting on that night, and abstinent from their wives on that night; and let the mass-priest sprinkle holy-water over them all, and let each of them taste of the holy water, and give them all the book and the image of Christ's rood to kiss. And let no man mend the fire any longer when the hallowing is begun; but let the iron lie upon the hot embers till the last collect; after that, let it be laid upon the 'stapela' [pile of wood], and let there be no other speaking within, except that they earnestly pray to Almighty God that He make manifest what is soothest. And let him go thereto; and let his hand be enveloped, and be it postponed till after the third day, whether it be foul or clean within the envelope. And he who shall break this law, be the ordeal with respect to him void, and let him pay to the king one hundred and twenty shillings as 'wite' [fine] — Laws of King Aethelstan, B. Thorpe, *Ancient Laws and Institutes.*

Servants, 960

If a woman give her maid a whipping with evil malice and if death is caused by the whipping and the maid be innocent, the mistress is to fast for 7 years. If, however, the maid was at fault, the mistress should fast for 3 years and should do penance for her sins — Canons enacted under King Edgar, 956-75, B. Thorpe, *Ancient Laws and Institutes of England.*

The Laws of Edgar, 962-963

2.1. And it is my will that secular rights be in force among the Danes according to as good laws as they can best decide on.

2.1a. Among the English, however, that is to be in force which I and my councillors have added to the decrees of my ancestors, for the benefit of all the nation.

2.2. Nevertheless, this measure is to be common to all the nation, whether Englishmen, Danes or Britons, in every province of my dominion, to the end that poor men and rich may possess what they rightly acquire, and a thief may not know where to dispose of stolen goods,

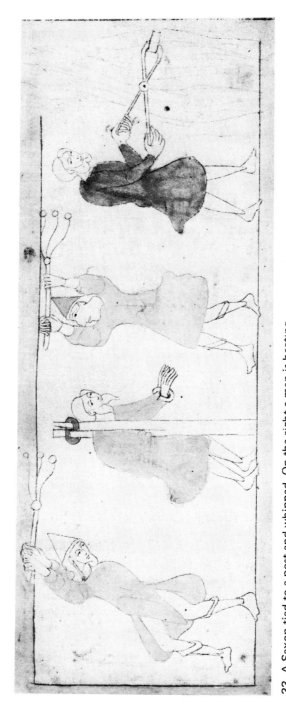

33. A Saxon tied to a post and whipped. On the right a man is heating a branding iron to brand the ill-doer.

although he steal anything, and against their will they be so guarded against, that few of them shall escape.

12. Further, it is my will that there should be in force among the Danes such good laws as they best decide on, and I have ever allowed them this and will allow it as long as my life lasts because of your loyalty, which you have always shown me.

12.1 And I desire that this one decree concerning such an investigation shall be common to us all, for the protection and security of all the nation.

13. And it is my will that villagers and their herdsmen may hold the same investigation among my livestock and among that of my thegns, as they hold among their own.

13.1 If then my reeve or any other man, in high or low position, refuses it, and offers indignity either to the villagers or their herdsmen, the Danes are to decide by law what punishment they wish to apply in that matter.

14. Among the English, I and my councillors have decided that the punishment shall be, if any man offers resistance or goes to the length of slaying any one of those who are concerned in this investigation and who inform about concealed cattle, or any of those who give true witness and by their truthfulness save the innocent and lawfully bring destruction upon the guilty.

14.1 It is, then, my will that what you have decided on for the improvement of public order, with great wisdom and in a way very pleasing to me, shall ever be observed among you.

14.2 And this addition to be common to all of us who inhabit these islands.

15. Now Earl Oslac and all the host who dwell in his ealdormanry are to give their support that this may be enforced, for the peace of God and the benefit of the souls of all of us and the security of all people.

15.1 And many documents are to be written concerning this, and sent both to Ealdorman Ælfhere and Ealdorman Æthelwine, and they are to send them in all directions, that this measure may be known to both the poor and the rich.

16. I will be a very gracious lord to you as long as my life lasts, and I am very well pleased with you all, because you are so zealous about the maintenance of the peace — The Laws of Edgar at 'Wihtbordesstan', translated by B. Thorpe, *English Historical Documents*, Vol. I.

Laws Concerning the Assembling of Councils, *c.* 970

(*a*) And let the 'hundred-gemot' [moot, meeting] be attended as it was before fixed; and thrice in the year let a 'burhgemot' be held; and twice a shire-gemot'; and let there be present the bishop of the shire and the 'Ealdorman,' and these both expound as well the law of God as the secular law.

(*b*) This is the ordinance how the hundred shall be held:

First, that they meet always within four weeks; and that every man do justice to another.

2. That a thief shall be pursued . . .

If there be present need, let it be made known to the hundred man, and let him [make it known] to the tithing men; and let all go forth to where God may direct them to go; let them do justice on the thief.

7. In the hundred, as in any other gemot, we ordain: that folk-right be pronounced in every suit, and that a term be fixed, when it shall be fulfilled. And he who shall break that term, unless it be by his lord's decree, let him make his 'bôt' [reparation] with XXX shillings, and on the day fixed, fulfil that which he ought to have done before.

8. An ox's bell, and a dog's collar, and a bleathorn; either of these three shall be worth a shilling, and each is reckoned an informer.

9. Let the iron that is for the threefold ordeal weigh III pounds; and for the single one pound – Laws of King Edgar, B. Thorpe, *Ancient Laws and Institutes.*

Charms

To recover stolen cattle, horses or goods.

A man must sing when one hath stolen any one of his cattle. Say before thou speak any other word. Bethlehem was hight the borough, wherein Christ was born: it is far famed over all earth. So may this deed be in sight of men notorious, per crucem Christi. Then pray three times to the east, and say thrice, May the cross of Christ bring it back from the east; and *turn* to the west, and say, May the cross of Christ bring it back from the west; and to the south, and say thrice, May the cross of Christ bring it back from the south; and to the north, and say, The cross of Christ was hidden and has been found. The Jews hanged Christ, they did to him the worst of deeds; they concealed what they were not able to conceal. So never may this deed become concealed. Per crucem Christi.

If cattle be taken away privily; if it be a horse, sing this over his foot shackles, or over his bridle. If it be another sort of cattle, sing over the hoof track, and light three candles and drip the wax three times into the hoof track. No man will be able to conceal it. If it be other goods, then sing it on the four sides of thee, and first sing it looking up. Peter, Patrick, Philip, Mary, Bridget, Felicitas; in the name of God, and the church; he who seeketh, findeth — from O. Cockayne, *Leechdoms, Wortcunning and Starcraft of Early England.*

Ordinance about Stolen Cattle

If any one pursue the track of stolen cattle from one 'staeth' [a station on the boundary river] to another, then let him commit the tracing to the men of the country or show by some mark that it is rightfully pursued. Let him then take to it who owns the land, and have the inquiry to himself, and 9 days afterwards compensate for the cattle, or deposit an 'underwed' [pledge] on that day, which shall be worth half as much again as the cattle; and in 9 days from that time let him redeem the 'wed' [pledge] by lawful payment. If it be said that the track is wrongfully pursued, then must he who traces the cattle lead to the 'staeth', and there himself one of six unchosen men, who are true, make oath that he according to folk-right [customary law] makes lawful claim on the land, as his cattle went thereup — Ordinance by the English witan and counsellors of the Welsh, B. Thorpe, *Ancient Laws and Institutes of England.*

Wrongdoers to be Destroyed, 1008

And if wizards or sorcerers, magicians or whores, murderers or perjurers are caught anywhere in the land, they are to be zealously driven out of this country, and this nation is to be purified, or they are to be completely destroyed in this country, unless they desist and atone very deeply — Laws of Ethelred (Ethelred VI), *English Historical Documents*, Vol. I.

The Laws of King Cnut, 1018

This is the ordinance which the councillors determined and devised according to many good precedents; and that took place as soon as King Cnut with the advice of his councillors completely established peace and friendship between the Danes and the English and put an end to all their former strife. In the first place, the councillors determined that above all things they would ever honour one God and steadfastly hold one Christian faith, and would love King Cnut with due loyalty and zealously observe Edgar's laws. And they agreed that they would, with God's help, investigate further at leisure what was necessary for the nation as best they could. Now we wish to make clear what can benefit us in religious and secular concerns, let him pay heed who will. Let us very resolutely turn from sins and eagerly atone for our misdeeds and duly love and honour one God and steadfastly hold one Christian faith and diligently avoid every heathen practice — The Laws of Cnut, *English Historical Documents*, Vol. I.

A Compilation on Status, *c*. 1002-1023

1. Once it used to be that people and rights [law] went by dignities, and councillors of the people were then entitled to honour, each according to his rank, whether noble or ceorl, retainer or lord.

2. And if a ceorl prospered, that he possessed fully five hides [about a hundred acres] of land of his own, a bell and a castle-gate, a seat and special office in the king's hall, then he was henceforth entitled to the rights of a thegn [one who retains the element of service rather than of high rank].

3. And the thegn who prospered, that he served the king and rode in his household band [the king's bodyguard] on his missions [important errands], if he himself had a thegn who served him, possessing five hides on which he discharged the king's dues [military service and

public charges] , and who attended his lord in the king's hall, and had thrice gone on his errand to the king — then he [the intermediate thegn] was afterwards allowed to represent his lord with his preliminary oath, and legally obtain his right to pursue a charge, wherever he needed.

4. And he who had no such distinguished representative, swore in person to obtain his rights, or lost his case.

5. And if a thegn prospered, that he became an earl, then was he afterwards entitled to an earl's rights.

6. And if a trader prospered, that he crossed thrice the open sea at his own expense, he was then afterwards entitled to the rights of a thegn.

7. And if there were a scholar who prospered with his learning so that he took orders and served Christ, he should afterwards be entitled to so much more honour and protection as belonged by rights to that order, if he kept himself chaste as he should.

8. And if anyone, anywhere, injured an ecclesiastic or a stranger by word or deed, then it was the concern of the bishop and the king, that they should atone for it as quickly as they could — C.C.C.C. MS. 201, a manuscript with connections with Archbishop Wulfstan of York, 1002-23.

Heathen Practice Forbidden, 1020-1023

5. And we earnestly forbid every heathen practice.
    5.1. It is heathen practice if one worships idols, namely if one worships heathen gods and the sun or the moon, fire or flood, wells or stones or any kind of forest trees, or if one practises witchcraft or encompasses death by any means, either by sacrifice or divination, or takes part in such delusions — Laws of Cnut, *English Historical Documents*, Vol. I.

12 Warfare

The Battle of Camlan, 539

On the other side, Arthur, too, was marshalling his army. He divided his men into nine divisions of infantry, each drawn up in a square, with a right and left wing. To each he appointed a commander. Then he exhorted them to kill these perjured villains and robbers who, at the request of one who had committed treason against him, the King, had been brought into the island from foreign parts to steal their lands from them. He told them, too, that this miscellaneous collection of barbarians, come from a variety of countries — raw recruits who were totally inexperienced in war — would be quite incapable of resisting valiant men like themselves, who were the veterans of many battles, provided always that they made up their minds to attack boldly and to fight like men.

While the two commanders were encouraging their men in this way in both the armies, the lines of battle suddenly met, combat was joined, and they all strove with might and main to deal each other as many blows as possible. It is heartening to describe what slaughter was inflicted on both sides, how the dying groaned, and how great was the fury of those attacking. Everywhere men were receiving wounds themselves or inflicting them, dying or dealing out death. In the end, when they had passed much of the day in this way, Arthur, with a single division in which he had posted six thousand, six hundred and sixty-six men, charged at the squadron where he knew Mordred was. They hacked a way through with their swords and Arthur continued to advance, inflicting terrible slaughter as he went. It was at this point that the accursed traitor was killed and many thousands of his men with him.

However, the others did not take to flight simply because Mordred was dead. They massed together from all over the battlefield and did their utmost to stand their ground with all the courage at their command. The battle which was now joined between them was fiercer than ever, for almost all the leaders on both sides were present and rushed into the fight at the head of their troops. On Mordred's side

34. A detail from a French manuscript showing, on the left, King Arthur in battle.

there fell Chelric, Elaf, Egbrict and Bruning, all of them Saxons; the Irishmen Gillapatric, Gillasel and Gillarvus, and the Scots and Picts, with nearly everyone in command of them. On Arthur's side there died Odbrict, King of Norway; Aschil, King of Denmark; Cador Limenich; and Cassivelaunus, with many thousands of the King's troops, some of them Britons, others from the various peoples he had brought with him. Arthur himself, our renowned King, was mortally wounded and was carried off to the Isle of Avalon, so that his wounds might be attended to. He handed the crown of Britain over to his cousin Constantine, the son of Cador Duke of Cornwall: this in the year 542 after our Lord's Incarnation – Geoffrey of Monmouth, *Historia Regum Brittanniae (The History of the Kings of Britain)*, translated by Lewis Thorpe.

Destruction of Britain in the Sixth Century

A vague rumour suddenly as if on wings reaches the ears of all, that their inveterate foes were rapidly approaching to destroy the whole country, and to take possession of it, as of old, from one end to the other. But yet they derived no advantage from this intelligence . . . A pestilential disease mortally affected the foolish people, which, without the sword, cut off so large a number of persons, that the living were not able to bury them. . . . A council was called to settle what was best and most expedient to be done, in order to repel such frequent and fatal irruptions and plunderings of the above-named nations.

Then all the councillors, together with that proud tyrant Gurthrigern (Vortigern), the British king, were so blinded, that, as a protection to their country, they sealed its doom by inviting in among them (like wolves into the sheep-fold), the fierce and impious Saxons, a race hateful both to God and men, to repel the invasions of the northern nations. Nothing was ever so pernicious to our country, nothing was ever so unlucky. What palpable darkness must have enveloped their minds – darkness desperate and cruel! Those very people whom, when absent, they dreaded more than death itself, were invited to reside, as one may say, under the selfsame roof – *The Works of Gildas,* translated by J.A. Giles in *Six Old English Chronicles.*

The Battle of Cuil Dremhni, 561

The monk Finnian of Moville visited Pope Pelagius, who reigned from 555 to 560, and first brought 'the whole Gospel to Ireland'. Columba borrowed it and transcribed it. Finnian was furious. The dispute went before King Diarmait, who decided in favour of Finnian, 'As a calf is to the cow, so is the copy to the book.'

Columba was a royal prince, the dynastic opponent of Diarmait. The monks were the king's enemies. A young man fled to Columba for protection. The king overruled his right pf sanctuary. The man was executed. Columba went to his home, Tir Connel, raised an army with king Ainmere and the king of Connacht, father of the dead man.

They gave battle to Diarmait and his army at Cuil Dremhni. Columba was present with his forces ... and besought God by prayer and fasts to grant victory over the insolent king without loss to his own men ... At the king's request, saint Finnian ... prayed for the royal army ... But the royal army was dispersed in flight, losing 3,000 men, their opponents losing one man only ... Columba made peace with the defeated king ... and kept the book — *vita Columbae.* From John Morris, *The Age of Arthur.*

'Columba had gone to war to vindicate the independence of the church, upholding the right of sanctuary against royal justice, denying the right of the king's law to forbid the free circulation of the word of God' — John Morris, *The Age of Arthur.*

The Fear that Columba Might Become Both Head of the Church and a Secular King

When the news of the battle came to the ears of the saints of Ireland, Columba was assailed as the author and occasion of so great a loss of life. A general meeting decided that it was proper for him to perform a solemn penance, to be determined by Saint Lasrian ... Lasrian enjoined him to leave Ireland and his family, and to spend the rest of his life in exile abroad, where he might win more souls for Christ than he had caused to die in battle. Columba sadly undertook the penance prescribed, saying to Lasrian 'So be it' — *vita Columbae.* From John Morris, *The Age of Arthur.*

Taliesin Celebrates the Last Northern British Victory over the English, 593

When Oswain slew Fflamddwyn
   It was no more than sleeping.
Sleeps now the wide host of England
   With the light upon their eyes
And those who fled not far
   Were braver than was need ...

Splendid he was, in his many coloured armour,
  Horses he gave to all who asked
Gathering wealth like a miser
  Freely he shared it for his soul's sake
The soul of Owain son of Urien
  May the Lord look upon its needs.

Taliesin, *Death Song to Owain*,
translated by Rachel Bromwich.

The Battle of Catraeth, 598, from the Best Known of Early Poems, the *Goddodin* of Aneirin

Mynydawc and Cynan led the Edinburgh British south towards Catterick hoping to join the Devians. This failed, and Aethelferth's English, in great numbers, annihilated the expeditionary force. Bede wrote, 'From that time forth no king of the Scots dared face the English in the field.'

Men went to Catraeth
Shouting for battle,
A squadron of horse.

Blue their armour and their shields,
Lances uplifted and sharp,
Mail and sword glinting . . .

Though they were slain, they slew.
None to his home returned . . .

Short their lives,
Long the grief
Among their kin.

Seven times their number,
The English they slew,
Many the women they widowed
Many the mothers who wept . . .

After the wine and after the mead
They left us, armoured in mail.
I know the sorrow of their death.

They were slain, they never grew grey . . .
From the army of Mynydawc, grief unbounded
Of three hundred men, but one returned.

From the *Goddodin Cycle* of poems.

Britons Resist the Mercians, *c.* 705

Thus it happened in the days of Cenred, king of the Mercians, when the Britons, the dangerous enemies of the Saxon race, were oppressing the nation of the English with war, pillage and devastation of the people, that on a certain night at the time of cockcrow, as the man of blessed memory, Guthlac, was devoting himself according to his wont to vigils and prayers, he was suddenly, as he supposed, overcome by sleep, and seemed to hear the shouts of a raging crowd. Then, in less time than it takes to tell it, roused from a light sleep, he went outside the little cell in which he was sitting, and standing, pricking up his ears, he recognized the words that the crowd were saying and that British hosts were approaching his cell. For in former vicissitudes of other times, he had been an exile among them, long enough to be able to understand their sibilant speech. They strove without delay to enter the house across the swamp, and almost at the same moment he saw all his buildings on fire, with the flame rising above them; him too they caught, and began to lift him up aloft on the sharp points of their spears. Then truly the man of God at length plainly perceived the thousand-fold shapes of the deceitful enemy with his thousand-fold wiles, and chanted as if with prophetic mouth the first verse of the 67th psalm: 'Let God arise.' When they heard this, all the hosts of demons, in less time than it takes to tell it, vanished at the same moment like smoke from his sight – *Life of St Guthlac,* by Felix, translated by D. Whitelock, *English Historical Documents*, Vol. I.

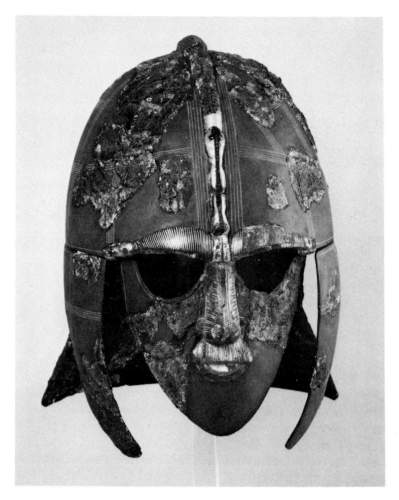

35. The Sutton Hoo helmet. The iron cap is covered with patterned bronze and has also silver and bronze-gilt decorations. The raised parts over the eyes are set with garnets. Seventh century. New reconstruction, 1971.

The Danish Invasions

787. In this year the king Beorhtic took to wife Eadburh, daughter of king Offa. And in his days came first three ships of Norweigians from Hörthaland [around Hardanger Fjord]; and then the reeve rode thither and tried to compel them to go to the royal manor, for he did not know

what they were; and then they slew him. These were the first ships of the Danes to come to England — *Anglo-Saxon Chronicle*, translated by G.N. Garmonsway.

The Viking Age: Their First Attack Falls on the Island of Lindisfarne, 793

The fourth year of King Ethelred, dreadful prodigies terrified the wretched nation of the English. For horrible lightnings and dragons in the air and fiery flashes were often seen to gleam and fly to and fro; and these signs signified a great famine and the fearful and indescribable slaughter of many men which followed.

In this year [793] also Ealdorman Sicga, who killed King Ælfwold, perished by his own hand, and his body was conveyed to the island of Lindisfarne on 23 April . . .

In the same year the pagans from the northern regions came with a naval force to Britain like stinging hornets and spread on all sides like fearful wolves, robbed, tore and slaughtered not only beasts of burden, sheep and oxen, but even priests and deacons, and companies of monks and nuns. And they came to the church of Lindisfarne, laid everything waste with grievous plundering, trampled the holy places with polluted steps, dug up the altars and seized all the treasures of the holy church. They killed some of the brothers, took some away with them in fetters, many they drove out, naked and loaded with insults, some they drowned in the sea . . .

794. The aforesaid pagans, ravaging the harbour of King Ecgfrith, plundered the monastery at the mouth of the River Don [Jarrow]. But St. Cuthbert did not allow them to go away unpunished; for their chief was killed by the English with a cruel death, and after a short space of time the violence of a storm battered, destroyed and broke to pieces their ships, and the sea overwhelmed many of them. Some were cast on the shore, and soon killed without mercy. And these things befell them rightly, for they had gravely injured those who had not injured them — Simeon of Durham, *History of the Church of Durham in 1104-1108.*

The Destruction of Northumbria, East Anglia and Mercia, 865-873

i. 865. In this year . . . a great heathen army came into England and took up winter quarters in East Anglia; and there they were supplied with horses, and the East Angles made peace with them.
ii. 866. In this year the army went from East Anglia to Northumbria, across the Humber estuary to the city of York. And there was great civil strife going on in that people, and they had deposed their king Osbert, and taken a king with no hereditary right, Aella. And not until late in the year did they unite sufficiently to proceed to fight the raiding army; and nevertheless they collected a large army and attacked the enemy in York, and broke into the city; and some of them got inside, and an immense slaughter was made of the Northumbrians, some inside and some outside, and both kings were killed, and the survivors made peace with the enemy.
iii. 869. In this year the raiding army rode across Mercia into East Anglia, and took up winter quarters at Thetford. And that winter King Edmund fought against them, and the Danes had the victory, and killed the king and conquered all the land, and destroyed all the monasteries to which they came.
iv. 873. In this year the army went from Lindsey to Repton and took up winter quarters there, and drove King Burgred across the sea, after he had held the kingdom 22 years. And they conquered all that land. . . . And the same year they gave the kingdom of the Mercians to be held by Ceolwulf, a foolish king's thegn; and he swore oaths to them and gave hostages, that it should be ready for them on whatever day they wished to have it, and he would be ready himself and all who would follow him, at the enemy's service — *Anglo-Saxon Chronicle, English Historical Documents,* Vol. I.

The Battle of Ashdown, 871

While the king Ethelred delayed long at his prayers, the Pagans, being fully prepared, arrived speedily at the place of conflict, and then Alfred, although second-in-command, when he could no longer sustain the assault of the foe, unless he either retreated from the fight or rushed on against his assailants before the arrival of his brother, led the

Christian troops against their opponents with the courage of a wild boar — Asser, *Life of King Alfred*, translated by L.C. Jane.

The Battle of Edington, 878

In this year in midwinter after twelfth night the enemy army came stealthily to Chippenham, and occupied the land of the West Saxons and settled there, and drove a great part of the people across the sea, and conquered most of the others; and the people submitted to them, except King Alfred. He journeyed in difficulties through the woods and fen-fastnesses with a small force ... And afterwards at Easter, King Alfred with a small force made a stronghold at Athelney, and he and the section of the people of Somerset which was nearest to it proceeded to fight from that stronghold against the enemy. ... And then ... he went ... to Edington and there fought against the whole army and put it to flight, and pursued it as far as the fortress, and stayed there a fortnight. And then the enemy gave him preliminary hostages and great oaths that they would leave his kingdom, and promised also that their king should receive baptism, and they kept their promise — *Anglo-Saxon Chronicle, English Historical Documents,* Vol. I.

The Fortification of a 'Burgh', 889-899

... at the request of Bishop Waerferth their friend, Ealdorman Ethelred and Aethelflaed ordered the borough of Worcester to be built for the protection of all the people, and also to exalt the praise of God therein. And they now make known, with the witness of God, in this charter that they will grant to God and St Peter and to the lord of that church half of all rights which belong to their lordship, whether in the market or in the street, both within the fortification and outside; that things may be more honourably maintained in that foundation and also that they may more easily help the community to some extent; and that their memory may be the more firmly observed in that place for ever, so long as obedience to God shall continue in that minister — *ninth-century Charter, English Historical Documents,* Vol. I.

Attack from Brittany, 914

In this year a great naval force came over here from the south from Brittany, and two earls, Ohter and Hroald, with them.

And they went west round the coast so that they arrived at the Severn estuary and ravaged in Wales everywhere along the coast where it suited them. And they captured Cyfeiliog, bishop of Archenfield [Herefordshire], and took him with them to the ships; and then King Edward ransomed him for 40 pounds.

Then after that all the army went inland, still wishing to go on a raid towards Archenfield. Then the men from Hereford and Gloucester and from the nearest boroughs met them and fought against them and put them to flight and killed the earl Hroald and the brother of Ohter, the other earl, and a great part of the army, and drove them into an enclosure and besieged them there until they gave them hostages (promising) that they would leave the king's dominion. And the king had arranged that men were stationed against them on the south side of the Severn estuary, from the west, from Cornwall, east as far as Avonmouth, so that they dared not attack the land anywhere on that side.

Yet they stole inland by night on two occasions – on the one occasion east of Watchet, on the other occasion at Porlock. Then on both occasions they were attacked, so that few of them got away – only those who could swim out to the ships. And then they remained out on the island of Steepholme until they became very short of food and many men had died of hunger because they could not obtain any food. Then they went from there to Dyfed, and from there to Ireland; and this was in the autumn.

And then after that in the same year, before Martinmas [11 November], King Edward went to Buckingham with his army, and stayed there four weeks, and made both the boroughs, on each side of the river, before he went away. And Earl Thurcetel came and accepted him as his lord, and so did all the earls and the principal men who belonged to Bedford, and also many of those who belonged to Northampton – *Anglo-Saxon Chronicle*, translated by Dorothy Whitelock, *English Historical Documents*, Vol. I.

The English Kingdoms at the beginning of the seventh century.

The Submission of the Danes, 917

Yet again after this, before Martinmas in the same year, King Edward
went with West Saxon levies to Colchester, and repaired and rebuilt the
fortress where it had been destroyed. Many people both from East
Anglia and Essex, who had previously been under Danish domination,
submitted to him: and the entire Danish host swore union with him,

that they wished all that he wished, protecting all that he protected, by sea and land. The host which owed allegiance to Cambridge independently chose him as lord: the treaty was ratified with oaths exactly as he drew it up — *Anglo-Saxon Chronicle, English Historical Documents,* Vol. I.

A Saxon Coat of Mail, 975

First of all the wet plain, extremely cold,
brought me forth from its interior.
I know in my thoughts that I am not made, by excellent skill,
from fleeces of wool or from hairs.
Woofs are not wound for me, nor have I a warp,
nor for me does a thread resound from the force of many strokes,
nor does the whirring shuttle glide over me,
nor shall weavers' rods strike me from anywhere.
The worms that deck the fine yellow cloth with embroidery
did not weave me by the skill that the fates have given them.
Nevertheless before men far and wide over the earth
I shall be called a pleasing garment.
Say truly, man skilled in clever thoughts
and wise in words, what this garment is.

Old English Riddle in *The Exeter Book,*
translated by W. S. Mackie, Early English Text Society, O.S.

Ealdorman Brihtnoth and the Battle of Maldon, 991

Then, [the Battle of Maldon 991] the messenger of the Vikings stood on the bank, he called sternly, uttered words, boastfully speaking the seafarers' message to the earl [Brihtnoth], as he stood on the shore. 'Bold seamen have sent me to you, and bade me say, that it is for you to send treasure quickly in return for peace, and it will be better for you all that you buy off an attack with tribute, rather than that men so fierce as we should give you battle. There is no need that we destroy each other, if you are rich enough for this. In return for the gold we are ready to make a truce with you. If you who are richest determine to redeem your people, and to give to the seamen on their own terms

36. The Picts built this castle at Mousa in the Shetland Islands. Its dry-stone walls are sixteen feet thick, this 'broch' has a staircase leading to six floors. With only one door, the building, standing on a rocky ledge, was considered impregnable.

wealth to win their friendship and make peace with us, we will betake us to our ships with the treasure, put to sea and keep faith with you.'

Brihtnoth lifted up his voice, grasped his shield and shook his supple spear, gave forth words, angry and resolute, and made him answer: 'Hear you, sea-rover, what this folk says! For tribute they will give you spears, poisoned point and ancient sword, such war gear as will profit you little in the battle. Messenger of the seamen, take back a message, say to your people a far less pleasing tale, how that there stands here with his troop an earl of unstained renown, who is ready to guard this realm, the home of Ethelred my lord, people and land; it is the heathen that shall fall in the battle. It seems to me too poor a thing that you should go with our treasure unfought to your ships, now that you have made your way thus far into our land. Not so easily shall you win tribute; peace must be made with point and edge, with grim battle-play before we give tribute . . . '

The wolves of slaughter pressed forward, they recked not for the water, that Viking host; West over the Blackwater, over the gleaming water they came with their bucklers, the seamen came to land with their linden shields. . . .

Then the heathen wretches cut him [Brihtnoth] down, and both the warriors who stood near by, Aelfroth and Wulfmaer, lay overthrown; they yielded their lives at their lord's side. . . .

Brihtwold spoke and grasped his shield (he was an old companion); he shook his ash-wood spear and exhorted the men right boldly: 'Thoughts must be the braver, heart more valiant, courage the greater as our strength grows less. Here lies our lord, all cut down, the hero in the dust. Long may he mourn who thinks now to turn from the battle-play. I am old in years; I will not leave the field, but think to lie by my lord's side, by the man I held so dear'— from *English and Norse Documents* translated by Margaret Ashdown, *English Historical Documents,* Vol. I.

Danegeld, 991

991. And in that year it was determined that tribute should first be paid to the Danish men because of the great terror they were causing along the coast. The first payment was 10,000 pounds. Archbishop Sigeric first advised that course – *Anglo-Saxon Chronicle, English Historical Documents,* Vol. I.

English Treachery

i. 992. And the king then entrusted the expedition to the leadership of Ealdorman Aelfric and Earl Thored and Bishop Aelfstan and Bishop Aescwig, and they were to try if they could entrap the Danish army anywhere at sea. Then Ealdorman Aelfric sent someone to warn the enemy, and then in the night before the day on which they were to have joined battle, he absconded by night from the army, to his own great disgrace and then the enemy escaped.

ii. 998. In this year the army turned back east into the mouth of the Frome, and there they went inland everywhere into Dorset as widely as they pleased; and the English army was often assembled against them, but as soon as they were to have joined battle, a flight was always instigated by some means, and always the enemy had the victory in the end.

iii. 1001. As soon as they joined battle the people gave way, and the Danes made a great slaughter there, and then overran the land — and ever their next raid was worse than the one before it . . . they went about as they pleased, and nothing withstood them, and no naval force on sea, nor land force dared go against them, no matter how far inland they went. It was in every way grievous, for they never ceased from their evil doing.

iv. 1003. Then a great English army was gathered from Wiltshire and from Hampshire, and they were going very resolutely toward the enemy. Then Ealdorman Aelfric was to lead the army, but he was up to his old tricks. As soon as they were so close that each army looked on the other, he feigned him sick and began retching to vomit, and said that he was taken ill, and thus betrayed the people whom he should have led.

v. 1011. All those disasters befell us through bad policy, in that they were never offered tribute in time nor fought against; but when they had done most to our injury, peace and truce was made with them; and for all this truce and tribute they journeyed none the less in bands everywhere, and harried our wretched people, and plundered and killed them — *Anglo-Saxon Chronicle, English Historical Documents*, Vol. I.

The Massacre of St Brice's Day at Oxford, 1002

In the year of the incarnation of our Lord 1004, the second indiction, in the 25th year of my reign, by the ordering of God's providence, I, Ethelred, governing the monarchy of all Albion, have made secure with the liberty of a privilege by the royal authority a certain monastery situated in the town which is called Oxford, where the body of the blessed Frideswide rests, for the love of the all-accomplishing God; and I have restored the territories which belong to that monastery of Christ with the renewal of a new title-deed; and I will relate in a few words to all who look upon this document for what reason it was done. For it is fully agreed that to all dwelling in this country it will be well known that, since a decree was sent out by me with the counsel of my leading men and magnates, to the effect that all the Danes who had sprung up in this island, sprouting like cockle amongst the wheat, were to be destroyed by a most just extermination, and this decree was to be put into affect even as far as death, those Danes who dwelt in the afore-mentioned town, striving to escape death, entered this sanctuary of Christ, having broken by force the doors and bolts, and resolved to make a refuge and defence for themselves therein against the people of the town and the suburbs; but when all the people in pursuit strove, forced by necessity, to drive them out, and could not, they set fire to the planks and burnt, as it seems, this church with its ornaments and its books. Afterwards, with God's aid, it was renewed by me and my subjects, and, as I have said above, strengthened in Christ's name with the honour of a fresh privilege, along with the territories belonging to it, and endowed with every liberty, regarding royal exactions as well as ecclesiastical dues — *Cartulary of St Frideswide, English Historical Documents,* Vol. I.

King Ethelred Offers to Pay Tribute to the Danish Army, 1006

Then after midsummer the great Danish fleet came to Sandwich, and did just as they were accustomed, ravaged, burnt and slew as they went. Then the king [Ethelred] ordered the whole nation from Wessex and Mercia to be called out, and they were out on military service against the Danish army the whole autumn, yet it availed no whit more than it had often done before; for in spite of it all, the Danish army went about as it pleased, and the English levy caused the people of the country every sort of harm, so that they profited neither from the native army nor the foreign army.

When winter approached, the English army went home, and the Danish army then came after Martinmas to its sanctuary, the Isle of Wight, and procured for themselves everywhere whatever they needed; and then towards Christmas they betook themselves to the entertainment waiting them, out through Hampshire into Berkshire to Reading; and always they observed their ancient custom, lighting their beacons as they went. They then turned to Wallingford and burnt it all, and were one night at Cholsey, and then turned along Ashdown to Cuckhamsley Barrow, and waited there for what had been proudly threatened, for it had often been said that if they went to Cuckhamsley, they would never get to the sea. They then went home another way. The English army was then gathered at the Kennet, and they joined battle there, and at once they put that troop to flight, and afterwards carried their booty to the sea. There the people of Winchester could see that army, proud and undaunted, when they went past their gate to the sea, and fetched themselves food and treasures from more than fifty miles from the sea.

Then the king had gone across the Thames, into Shropshire, and received there his food-rents in the Christmas season. Then so great terror of the Danish army arose that no one could think or conceive how to drive them from the country, or to defend this country from them, for they had cruelly left their mark on every shire of Wessex with their burning and their harrying. The king then with his councillors began eagerly to consider what might seem to them all most advisable, that this country could be saved before it was completely destroyed. Then the king and his councillors, for the benefit of the whole nation, determined — hateful though it was to all of them — that tribute must needs be paid to the army. Then the king sent to the army to inform them that he desired that there should be a truce between them, and that tribute should be paid them and provisions given; and then they all accepted that, and they were supplied with food throughout England — *Anglo-Saxon Chronicle, English Historical Documents,* Vol. I.

Olaf the Stout Breaks Through London Bridge, 1009

Olaf had large hurdles made of withies and soft wood, so cut as to make a wicker-house, and thus covered his ships, so that the hurdles reached out over their sides; he had posts put beneath them so high that it was easy to fight beneath them, and the covering was proof against stones thrown on it. When the host was ready they rowed up the river; as they came near the bridges they were shot at, and such large stones thrown down on them that neither their helmets nor shields could withstand them; and the ships themselves were greatly damaged, and many retreated. But Olaf and the Northmen with him rowed up under the bridges, and tied ropes round the supporting posts and rowed their ships down stream as hard as they could. The posts were dragged along the bottom until they were loosened from under the bridges. As an armed host stood thickly on the bridges, and there was a great weight of stones and weapons upon them, and the posts beneath were broken, the bridges fell with many of the men into the river; the others fled into the city, or into Southwark. After this they attacked Southwark, and captured it — *The Saga of St Olaf* (King Olaf), from R.R. Sellman, *The Vikings.*

Once Again Swein, King of the Danes, Greatly Damages this Country, 1013

In the year after the archbishop was martyred, the king [Ethelred] appointed Bishop Lifing to the archbishopric of Canterbury. And in this same year, before the month of August, King Swein came with his fleet to Sandwich, and then went very quickly round East Anglia into the mouth of the Humber, and so up along the Trent until he reached Gainsborough. And then at once Earl Uhtred and all the Northumbrians submitted to him, as did all the people of Lindsey, and then all the people belonging to the district of the Five Boroughs, and quickly afterwards all the Danish settlers [the army] north of Watling Street, and hostages were given to him from every shire.

When he perceived that all the people had submitted to him, he gave orders that his army should be provisioned and provided with horses, and then he afterwards turned southward with his full forces and left the ships and the hostages in charge of his son Cnut. When he had crossed the Watling Street, they did the greatest damage that any army could do. He then turned to Oxford, and the citizens at once submitted and gave hostages; and from there to Winchester, where they did the same. He then turned eastward to London, and many of his host were drowned in the Thames because they did not trouble to find a bridge. When he came to the borough the citizens would not yield, but resisted with full battle, because King Ethelred was inside and Thorkel with him.

Then King Swein turned from there to Wallingford, and so west across the Thames to Bath, where he stayed with his army . . . He then turned northward to his ships, and all the nation regarded him as full king. And after that the citizens of London submitted and gave hostages, for they were afraid that he would destroy them. Then Swein demanded full payment and provisions for his army that winter, and Thorkel demanded the same for the army which lay at Greenwich, and in spite of it all they ravaged as often as they pleased. Nothing therefore was of benefit to this nation, neither from the south nor from the north.

Then King Ethelred was for a time with the fleet which lay in the Thames, and the queen went across the sea to her brother Richard, and with her Abbot Ælfsige, and the king sent Bishop Aelfhun across the sea with the athelings Edward and Alfred, that he should take care of them. And the king then went from the fleet to the Isle of Wight at

Christmas and spent that festival there; and after the festival went across the sea to Richard and was there with him until the happy event of Swein's death [1014] — *Anglo-Saxon Chronicle, English Historical Documents*, Vol. I.

13 England and the Sea

A Warning of Disaster, its Cause Explained after the Death of Offa of Mercia, 796

An immense threat hangs over this island and its people. It is a novelty without precedent that the pirate raids of a heathen people can regularly waste our shores. Yet the English people are divided, and king fights against king. Saddest of all, scarcely any heir of the ancient royal houses survives, and the origin of kings is as dubious as their courage ... Study Gildas, the wisest of the British, and examine the reasons why the ancestors of the British lost their kingdom and their fatherland; then look upon yourselves, and will find amongst you almost identical causes — Alcuin of York and Tours. From John Morris, *the Age of Arthur.*

The Battle of Aclea, 851

In English history, the first recorded naval battle.

851. In this year ... for the first time, heathen men stayed through the winter on Thanet. And the same year 350 ships came into the mouth of the Thames and stormed Canterbury and London and put to flight Brihtwulf, king of the Mercians, with his army, and went South across the Thames into Surrey. And King Æthelwulf and his son · Æthelbald fought against them at Aclea with the army of the West Saxons, and there inflicted the greatest slaughter on a heathen army that we have ever heard of until this present day, and had the victory there.

And the same year King Athelstan and Ealdorman Ealhere fought in ships and slew a great army at Sandwich in Kent, and captured nine ships and put others to flight — *Anglo-Saxon Chronicle, English Historical Documents,* Vol. I.

King Alfred's Navy, 896

896. Then King Alfred had long-ships built to oppose the Danish warships. They were almost twice as long as the others. Some had 60 oars, some more. They were both swifter and steadier and also higher than the others. They were built neither on the Frisian nor the Danish pattern, but as it seemed to him himself that they could be most useful. Then on a certain occasion of the same year six ships came to the Isle of Wight and did great harm there. . . . Then the king ordered a force to go thither with nine of the new ships, and they blocked the estuary from the seaward end. Then the Danes went out against them with three ships, and three were on dry land farther up the estuary; the men from them had gone upon land. Then the English captured two of those three ships at the entrance to the estuary and killed the men, and the one ship escaped. On it also the men were killed except five. These got away because the ships of their opponents ran aground. Moreover they had run aground very awkwardly: three were aground on that side of the channel on which the Danish ships were aground, and all the others on the other side, so that none of them could get to the others. But when the water had ebbed many furlongs from the ships, the Danes from the remaining three ships went to the other three which were stranded on their side, and they then fought there. . . . Then, however, the tide reached the Danish ships before the Christians could launch theirs, and therefore they rowed away out. . . . That same summer no fewer than 20 [Danish] ships, men and all perished along the south coast – *Anglo-Saxon Chronicle, English Historical Documents,* Vol. I.

Harrying Voyages of the Vikings, *c.* 1000

When Hacon was but a few winters old, Swein Asleif's son offered to take him as his foster child, and he was bred up there [the Orkneys], and as soon as ever he was so far fit, that he could go about with other men, the Swein had him away with him a sea-roving every summer, and led him to worthiness in everything.

It was Swein's wont at that time that he sat through the winter at home in Gairsay, and there he kept always about him eight men at his beck. He had so great a drinking-hall, that there was not other as great in all the Orkneys.

Swein had in the spring hard work, and made them lay down very

37. Gokstad, Vestfold, Norway. 'The Gokstad ship, above, and her kind
were the culmination of a long process of experiment which began at
least as far back as the Bronze Age, can be charted with fair accuracy
from the fourth to the seventh century, and found the right answers,
particularly in respect of bow, stem, and keel, and the all-important
business of mast and sail, in the eighth. The Gokstad ship is the perfect
example of her kind of ship, where proportion, construction, purpose
are fully harmonized' — Gwyn Jones. A replica, made in 1813, later
crossed the Atlantic in 28 days.

much seed, and looked much after it himself. But when that toil was ended he fared away every spring on a viking voyage, and harried about the Southern Isles and Iceland, and came home after mid-summer. That he called spring-viking. Then he was at home until the cornfields were reaped down, and the grain seen to, and stored. Then he fared away on a viking voyage, and then he did not come home until the winter was one month spent, and that he called his autumn-viking.

38. A monk going in a fishing-boat to the island of Crowland in the marshes of Lincolnshire. Tenth century.

On the spring cruise they had five ships with oars and all of them large. They harried about among the Southern Isles. Then the folk were so scared at him in the Southern Isles that men hid all their goods and chattels in the earth or in piles of rocks.

Swein sailed as far south as Man [Isle of Man], and got ill for spoil. But when they came about south under Dublin, then two keels sailed from there off the main, which had come from England and meant to steer for Dublin; they were laden with English cloths, and great store of goods were aboard them.

Swein and his men pulled up to the keels, and offered them battle. Little came of the defence of the Englishmen before Swein gave the word to board. Then the Englishmen were made prisoners. And then they robbed them of every penny which was aboard the keels, save that the Englishmen kept the clothes they stood in and some food, and went on their way afterwards with the keels, but Swein and his men fared to the Southern Isles, and shared their war spoil.

They sailed from the west with great pomp. They did this as a glory for themselves when they lay in harbours, that they threw awnings of English cloth over their ships. But when they sailed into the Orkneys they sewed the cloth on to the forepart of the sails, so that it looked in that wise as though the sails were made altogether of broadcloth. This they called the broadcloth cruise. Swein fared home to his house in Gairsay. He had taken from the keels much wine and English mead – *Icelandic Sagas,* Vol. III. *The Orkneyingers' Saga,* translated by G.W. Dasent. Rolls Series.

Select Bibliography

Arnold, Ralph. *A Social History of England, 55 B.C. to A.D. 1215.* Constable

Barlow, F. *The English Church 1000-1066.* Longmans

Brondsted, J. *The Vikings.* Penguin

Brooke, C.N.L. *From Alfred to Henry III: 871-1272.* Nelson

Brooke, C.N.L. *Saxon and Norman Kings.* Collins

Bruce-Mitford, R.L.S. *The Sutton Hoo Ship Burial. A Provincial Guide.* British Museum

Chadwick, H.M. *The Heroic Age.* Cambridge University Press

Clapham, A.W. *English Romanesque Architecture before the Conquest.* Oxford University Press

Darby, H.C. *A Historical Geography of England.* Cambridge University Press

Deanesly, M. *The Pre-Conquest Church in England.* Black

Dolley, R.H.M. *Anglo-Saxon Coins.* Methuen

Duckett, E.S. *Anglo-Saxon Saints and Scholars.* Macmillan

Duckett, E.S. *Alfred the Great and his England.* Collins

Duckett, E.S. *Saint Dunstan of Canterbury.* Collins

Fox, C. *Offa's Dyke.* Oxford University Press

Garmonsway, G.N. *Anglo-Saxon Chronicle.* Everyman's Library

Gordon, R.K. *Anglo-Saxon Poetry* (translation). Everyman's Library

Gray, H.L. *English Field-Systems.* Merlin Press

Hodgkin, R.H. *A History of the Anglo-Saxons.* Oxford University Press

Hoskins, W.G. *The Making of the English Landscape.* Hodder and Stoughton

Hunter-Blair, P. *An Introduction to Anglo-Saxon England.* Cambridge University Press

Jessup, R. *Anglo-Saxon Jewellery.* Faber

John, E. *Land Tenure in Early England.* Leicester University Press

Jolliffe, J.E.A. *Pre-Feudal England: the Jutes.* Oxford University Press

Kendrick, T.D. *Anglo-Saxon Art to A.D. 900.* Methuen

Kendrick, T.D. *Late Saxon and Viking Art.* Methuen

Kirby, D.P. *The Making of Early England.* Batsford

Knowles, M.D. *The Monastic Order in England.* Cambridge University Press

Larson, L.M. *Cnut the Great.* Madison

Levison, W. *England and the Continent in the Eighth Century.* Oxford University Press

Marsh, Henry. *Dark Age Britain.* David and Charles

Orwin, C.S. *The Open Fields.* Oxford University Press

Page, R.I. *Life in Anglo-Saxon England.* Batsford

Plummer, C. *The Life and Times of Alfred the Great.* Oxford University Press

Quennell, M. and C.H.B. *Everyday Life in Anglo-Saxon, Viking, and Norman Times.* Batsford

Sayles, G.O. *The Medieval Foundations of England.* Methuen

Sherley-Price, L. (translation). *Bede: A History of the English Church and People.* Penguin

Stenton, F.M. *Anglo-Saxon England.* Oxford University Press

Tait, J. *The Medieval English Borough.* Manchester University Press

Whitelock, D. *The Beginnings of English Society.* Penguin

Whitelock, D. *English Historical Documents, c. 500-1042* (Volume I). Eyre and Spottiswoode

Wilson, D.M. *The Anglo-Saxons.* Thames and Hudson

Biographies

(These are the authors of material in this book, and also some famous men to whom these authors were indebted.)

Aelfric, called *Grammaticus* (*c.* 955-1020), a monk at Winchester and Cerne Abbas, and abbot of Eynsham. He drew on the works of St Augustine, St Jerome and St Gregory for his *Catholic Homilies.* His *Lives of the Saints,* with their alliterative rhythms, were suitable for reading aloud on festivals. He compiled a Latin grammar, and a *Colloquy* between a master, his pupils and men of different callings. This was designed to teach schoolboys conversational Latin. Aelfric also translated into English the first seven books of the Old Testament, and wrote a treatise, *De Veteri et de Novo Testamento,* an introduction to the Testaments. He was the greatest prose writer of his time, and showed clearly 'the belief and practice of the early English Church'.

Aethelbert, also *Ethelbert* (552-616), king of Kent. By 590 he had gained the hegemony over England south of the Humber. In his reign Christianity was introduced by St Augustine. We owe to this king the first written English Laws.

Aethelred the Unready, king of England, 979-1016. He was seven when his father King Edgar died, and ten when the murder in 979 of his half-brother Edward the Martyr made him king. He was influenced by unworthy favourites; 'Unready' is properly 'Rede-less', the man without counsel. His reign was a series of raids by the Danes, and attempts to buy them off with Danegeld levies. Aethelred's laws show that theft continued to preoccupy kings of England. In 1002 he married Emma, the daughter of Duke Richard of Normandy; their son became Edward the Confessor.

Aethelstan or *Athelstan,* king of England 925-40, grandson of King Alfred. He did much towards the unification of the English people, and showed his strength by defeating the Welsh, Scots and Danes at Brunanburh in 937. His policy tended to bring England closer to the Continent. His sister married Otho the Great, afterwards emperor;

another sister married Hugh the Great, Duke of the Franks, father of Hugo Capet. At home he improved the laws, built monasteries, and promoted commerce. 'Many of the cultural changes which are commonly attributed to the Norman Conquest can be traced back to Aethelstan's reign.'

Aethelweard or *Ethelward*, historian, was the great-grandson of Aethelred, and ealdorman of Wessex. His Latin *Chronicle* extends to the year 975. In this work he is largely dependent on the *Anglo-Saxon Chronicle* up to 892. He was a friend and patron of Aelfric.

Aethelwold or *Ethelwold, St* (908-84), born at Winchester, entered Glastonbury monastery, was a pupil of St Dunstan the abbot, and became dean. Later he re-established a monastic house at Abingdon, and introduced St Benedict's Rule from Fleury. He was a personal friend of King Edgar, and persuaded him to expel the married clergy from Winchester, Chertsey, Milton and Ely and introduce monks in their place. He rebuilt the church of Peterborough, and built a new cathedral at Winchester. He wrote *Regularis Concordia,* a collection of regulations and customs of Benedictine convents. The colouring of Aethelwold's *Benedictional* is 'the most sumptuous of the surviving late Saxon manuscripts'.

Alcuin or *Albinus* of York (735-804), born at York, was educated in the cloister school of York under Archbishop Egbert, and was in charge of the library, said to be the finest north of the Alps. He met the Emperor Charlemagne at Parma in 781, and was called in to reorganise Frankish education and scholarship. Finally, he became abbot of Tours. Alcuin wrote liturgical and philosophical works, many letters and poems, and was sharply critical of the behaviour of English monks. His Latin elegy tells of the destruction of Lindisfarne by the Danes.

Aldheim, St (640-709), a West Saxon, educated first by an Irish monk at Malmesbury, then at Canterbury under Theodore. His Latin works, including some praising the merits of virginity, showed wide knowledge of classic authors, and were highly praised, though his style was ornate and involved, with many archaic words. Bede ranked him as a great historian. In 689 he sent a famous letter 'On Virginity' to Hildelith, Abbess of Barking, describing her and her nuns as 'spiritual athletes'. He was abbot of Malmesbury, built churches there and at Bruton and Wareham, monasteries at Frome and Bradford in Wessex.

Alfred (849-901), king of the West Saxons 871-901, revived interest in literature in the west of England. To improve the education of the clergy he translated Pope Gregory's *Cura Pastoralis*. Here his preface touches on the decay of learning in Wessex. He then translated the *Historia adversus Paganos* of Orosius, giving accounts from the explorers Ohthere to the White Sea and from Wulfstan in the Baltic. Bede's *Historia Ecclesiastica* was translated under his encouragement. Alfred also translated the *De Consolatione Philosophiae* of Boëthius, and part of St Augustine's unfinished *Soliloquies*; all these works place Christianity in world history. His code of laws collected the best among the enactments of former kings. The earlier part of the *Anglo-Saxon Chronicle* down to 892 may represent the work of King Alfred, or his help in the work. As a leader, his great work was in repelling the Danes, who threatened the whole country, and in helping towards the consolidation of England as his rule extended from Wessex to Northumbria.

Asser (d. 909), a monk of St David's, came from Wales and was persuaded to spend six months in every year at King Alfred's household and help in his studies, *c.* 885. He received the monasteries of Amesbury and Banwell, and became bishop of Sherborne. He is known for his Latin *Life of Alfred,* which is important as 'the earliest biography of an English laymen'.

Bede or *Baeda* (673-735), scholar and historian, studied at the Benedictine monastery under Benedict Biscop, abbot of Monkwearmouth in Durham. Then he was transferred to the twin monastery of Jarrow, and spent most of his life there. His industry was outstanding. Besides Greek and Latin, classical as well as patristic literature, he studied Hebrew, medicine, prosody and astronomy. He wrote homilies, hymns, epigrams, lives of saints, commentaries on the Old and New Testament. He was known as 'Venerable' a century after his death. His most valuable work is the *Historia Ecclesiastica Gentis Anglorum*, 'a wonderfully alive tapestry of Saxon England and Celtic Britain down to A.D. 731'. Bede is the greatest name in the ancient literature of England.

Benedict, St (480-543), the founder in 529 of the monastery on Monte Cassino in Campania. Of the Great Western Church orders it was the first in fame, and became the richest and most learned in Italy. St Benedict's *Regula Monachorum* became the accepted rule of all Western monachism, and led eventually, as Ralph Arnold says, 'to monasteries with fine churches and landed endowments, centres of learning, culture, and hospitality, and power-houses of religion'.

Caedmon (fl. 670). When an elderly man, he came to the monastery of Streaneshalch (Whitby), between 658 and 670, as a herdsman. Bede tells us how this man, sleeping in the convent's stable, suddenly in a vision, received the power of song, woke and composed nine lines about the Creation, in the metre of popular English songs of the day. The Abbess Hilda was delighted to hear the song. Then Caedmon turned many passages from the Scriptures into verse. *The Hymn to the Creator* is the only one of his poems to have survived.

Cnut or *Canute,* a Dane, king of England 1016-35. He divided the kingdom into the four earldoms of Mercia, Northumberland, Wessex and East Anglia. After the constant fighting to conquer this country he became a restrained ruler. Cnut restored the equal rights known in Edgar's time, and gradually replaced Danish earls with Anglo-Saxons. He himself married Emma, the widow of Ethelred. The death of his brother Harold in 1018 gave him the crown of Denmark; that of Olaf in 1030 the throne of Norway.

Columba, St, otherwise Columcille or Columbanus (521-97), son of Feidilmid, an Ulster chief, and a pupil of St Finnian at Molville on Strangford Lough and of another St Finnian at Clonard. He became a recluse at Glasnevin, and built churches at Derry and Durrow. The belief that he had caused the battle of Culdremhue in 561 led to excommunication and exile. He went with disciples to West Scotland, founded a monastery on Iona off the coast in 563, and from Iona converted the Northern Picts to Christianity. An *Altus* published by Dr Todd in the *Liber Hymnorum* has been ascribed to him, and other works are venerated in Ireland.

Cummean, (d. 662), the first Irish penitential writer to distinguish clearly between the varied conditions of men. He names a number of different grades in the Church, the bishop, priest, deacon, monk, and those not in orders. The principle of his sophisticated penitential is that the eight chief vices, avarice, gluttony, fornication, sloth, anger, dejection, vainglory and pride, are to be healed by their contrary virtues.

Cynewulf, probably lived in the latter part of the eighth century in Mercia. His name is known because in the concluding lines of four poems, *Juliana, Crist, Elene* and *The Fates of the Apostles*, it is worked into the text in runic characters, a kind of signature. These poems were contained in the 'Exeter Book' and the 'Vercelli Book', a codex of Old English manuscripts, in the chapter of Vercelli in north Italy. *Elene* is Cynewulf's finest poem.

Eadmer (d. 1124), a learned monk of Canterbury, who wrote *Historia Novorum in Anglia*, a Latin chronicle of events of his own day down to 1122, and a biography of his friend and leader, Archbishop Anselm, to whom he had been sent by Pope Urban.

Eadric, king of Kent; some of his laws were recorded beween 673 and 685.

Eddi, lived in the seventh century, when stone churches began to be built in Northumbria. He wrote a 'Life of St Wilfrid' and described Ripon Church as 'a church of dressed stone, supported by various columns and side aisles', and he praised Hexham with 'its crypts of wonderfully dressed stone and the manifold buildings above ground supported by various columns and many side aisles'.

Edgar, king of England, 959-75, was the younger son of Edmund. In 957 he became ruler of Northumbria and Mercia, dividing the realm with his brother Eadwig. On Eadwig's death in 959, Edgar became king of Wessex also, so uniting the whole country.

Edmund, king of the English, 939-46, following Aethelstan of whom it was said, 'through God's grace he alone ruled all England which before him many kings had held between them.' King Edmund's Laws forbade men in Holy Orders to marry; and made the payment of tithes enforceable for the first time by law.

Egbert, Archbishop of York, in 734 received a letter from Bede, his former teacher, saying sharp things about monasteries whose monks failed to follow a regular life and were 'useful neither to God nor to man'. The *Dialogue of Archbishop Egbert of York* speaks of the position when the slayer of an ecclesiastic cannot pay the wergild and declares he should be handed over to the king for punishment 'lest the slayers of the servants of God should think that they can sin with impunity'.

Felix, a Burgundian bishop, intent on missionary work, came to Canterbury and was sent by Archbishop Honorius to work in East Anglia. He asked for the help of schoolmasters for the school he wanted to start in Dunwich. He was made the first bishop of Dunwich, 631-47.

Florence of Worcester (d. 1118), a monk of Worcester, who wrote *Chronicon ex Chronicis* based on the work of Marianus, an Irish monk) coming down to 1117. The chronicle from about 1030 is held to be of value as first-hand information.

Frideswide, St (d. 735), an abbess and patroness of Oxford, daughter of Dida, an ealdorman. She founded the abbey which became Christ Church, Oxford. She was canonised in 1481.

Geoffrey of Monmouth, Gaufridus Monemutensis (1100-54), Benedictine monk of Monmouth, studied at Oxford, later in service of Robert, earl of Gloucester. He became bishop of St Asaph in 1152. His *Historia Regum Britanniae* presents 'the kings who dwelt in Britain before the incarnation of Christ' and many others who followed after. For Geoffrey his history was a pageant of vivid personalities moving towards the greatest of them all, Arthur son of Utherpendragon and Ygerna. 'Here,' said Professor Lewis Jones, 'was just what a romantic age was thirsting for, and Arthur immediately became the central figure of the most popular and most splendid of the romantic cycles . . . a hero whose deeds challenged comparison with those of Alexander and Charlemagne.'

Gildas, a Welsh scholar-bishop, who wrote in Latin shortly before 547 his tract, *De Excidio et Conquestu Britanniae,* having lived through the sixth-century events he describes. It is the only contemporary account here, after the Romans had left. The sufferings of the Britons at the hands of Picts, Scots and Saxons 'figure only incidentally as illustrations of God's methods of punishing backsliders'.

Gregory of Tours (*c.* 540-94), bishop of Tours. His *Historiarum sive Annalium Francorum* is the chief authority for the history of Gaul in the sixth century.

Gregory I, St, 'The Great', Pope 590-604, one of the greatest of the early popes, a most zealous propagator of Christianity. He was renowned for his administration, for the complete organisation of public services and ritual, for reforming and standardising the chant. He sent Augustine to England, and was the author of the *Cura Pastoralis, Dialogues, Letters,* homilies.

Henry of Huntingdon (1084-1155), a pupil of Bloet, bishop of Lincoln, became archdeacon of Huntingdon. His *Historia Anglorum* goes down to 1154, and contains a number of popular songs and stories taken from earlier works.

Hlothhere, king of Kent, whose laws were recorded between 673 and 685. One law decreed that a buyer must always make a purchase before reputable witnesses so that 'if the transaction were challenged the witnesses could be called upon to testify that the buyer had acted in good faith.'

Holinshed, Raphael (d. 1580). His *Chronicles* consist of a description of England followed by a history down to the Conquest; a description of Ireland and a chronicle; a description of Scotland and a history down to 1575; the history of the English kings to 1577. These, known by his name, include the work of other writers.

Hucbald or Hubaldus (c. 840-930), a Benedictine monk and writer on music, was born at the monastery of Saint Amand near Tournai. Between 883 and 900 Hucbald went on several missions reforming various schools of music. *Harmonica Institutio* is positively ascribed to him. He wrote numerous lives of the saints, and a curious poem on bald men, dedicated to Charles the Bald.

Ine or *Ina,* West Saxon king from 688 to 726. The Laws of Ine have survived because King Alfred appended a copy of them to his own code of laws. One of them says: 'If a man from a distance, or a stranger, journey away from a road, and he then neither shouts nor blows a horn, he is to be assumed to be a chief, to be either slain or redeemed.'

Llywarch Hen, sixth-century Welsh poet. The eastern and central part of ancient Wales, afterwards called *Powys*, 'settlement', had been greatly affected by Roman influences, shown in epigrammatic verse developed from the Latin elegiac couplet, and known as *englynion*. Such Welsh poetry was assigned to Llywarch Hen. It is elegiac, a lament for friends or lost glory, and describes desolation and solitude.

Matthew of Westminster, long supposed to be the author of *Flores Historiarum,* is 'an entirely imaginary person'. The earlier part is based on the *Chronica Majora* of Matthew Paris, and the oldest manuscript at one time was kept at Westminster Abbey. Because of these facts, the two names were combined as above.

Migne, Jacques Paul (1800-75), a French priest who set up a large publishing house at Petit Montrouge about 1836, from which came many theological works, including his *Patrologiae Cursus Completus* in 383 volumes.

Oswald of Worcester, St (d. 992), was nephew of Archbishop Oda, who sent him to study the new monasticism at the great abbey of Fleury-sur-Loire, where he became a Benedictine monk. He went with Oskitel, Archbishop of York, to Rome. Guided by St Dunstan, he became bishop of Worcester in 961, and helped in the revival of religion and learning, founding monasteries at Westbury, Worcester, Winchcombe, and the Isle of Ramsey. In 972 Oswald was promoted to Archbishop of York.

Roger of Wendover (d. 1236), a prior of the Benedictine monastery of St Albans. He wrote *Flores Historiarum,* which deals with the history of the world from the Creation to 1235.

Simeon of Durham (*c.* 1070-1138), chronicler, precentor of Durham. He wrote *Historia Ecclesiae Dunelmensis* and *Historia Regum Anglorum et Danorum.* The information for this 'History of the Kings' is thought to have come from a lost Northumbrian annal.

Taliesin (*fl.* 550), a Welsh bard, possibly mythical, first mentioned in the 'Saxon Genealogies' appended to the *Historia Britonum, c.* 690. In Wales in the sixth and seventh centuries lived several bards, the best known by name are Llywarch Hen, Taliesin and Aneirin, none of whom mention King Arthur. Poems attributed to these are found in manuscripts dated from the twelfth to the fourteenth centuries. To the thirteenth century belongs *The Book of Taliesin.* The village of Taliesin in Cardiganshire stands near the supposed site of his grave.

Theodore (602-90), Archbishop of Canterbury; born at Tarsus in Cilicia, studied at Athens, widely read in Greek and Latin literature. In 668 he was consecrated Archbishop of Canterbury by Pope Vitalius.

He founded a school of learning specialising in Greek at Canterbury, and created many bishoprics. Stubbs described him as the 'real organizer of the administrative system of the English Church', effects of which still survive. He was part author of the *Penitential*.

William of Malmesbury (*c*. 1095-1143), historian, was educated at Malmesbury Abbey, and became librarian and precentor there. His *Gesta Regum Anglorum* gives the history of kings of England from 449 to 1127; its sequel *Historia Novella* continues English history to 1142. The *Gesta Pontificum Anglorum* tells of the bishops and chief monasteries of England to 1125. His other works are *De Antiquitate Glastoniensis Ecclesiae* and a Life of St Dunstan. He had many of the highest qualifications of a historian: learning, judgment and a wide knowledge of the world.

Wulfstan or *Wolstan, St* (d. 1023), Archbishop of York, author of homilies in English, including the rousing sermon, *Sermo Lupi ad Anglos*, 1014, ascribing the disasters of the Danish conquest to the vices and demoralisation of all classes of Englishman.

Index

Felix, Bishop of Dunwich 148
Finns 82-4
fire, destruction by 27-9, 30
Florence of Worcester 22-3, 91-3
Flores Historiarum 17, 18-19, 96-7
Flowers of History see previous entry
food and drink 40-3
funerals 47, 118-19, 122-3

Garrick, compiler of *A Collection of
   Old Plays* 72
Geoffrey of Monmouth 11, 143-5
Gesta Regum Anglorum 17-18
gifts 17-19
Gildas, author 11-13, 99, 145
Giles, J.A., author and translator 145
Gnomic verses 68-9
Goddodin Cycle 147-8
Grammaticus *see* Aelfric
Gregory the Great, Pope 59, 95-7,
   100
Gregory of Tours 44
Guthfrith, King 16

Hardacnut, King 22-3, 91-3
Harold Harefoot, King 22-3
health 75-81
Hell 98-9, 109-11
Henry of Huntingdon 20-1
herbs 75, 77-9
'Hermit's Hut, The' 65-6
Historia Britonum 13
*Historia Ecclesiastica Gentis Anglo-
   rum* 9, 27-9, 40, 46, 58, 94-5,
   100-3, 104-9
Historia Regum 30-1
Historia Regum Brittanniae 143-5
History of St Cuthbert 16
History of the Church of Durham
   150
History of the Franks 44
History of the Kings of Britain see
   Historia Regum Brittanniae
Hlothhere, King of Kent 13-14,
   126-7
Holinshed, Raphael, English chronic-
   ler 84
Holy Days 114, 122
Hugh the Great, Duke of the Franks
   17-18
hunting 82-4
'Hymn to the Creator' 58
hymns 58, 59-60

Icelandic Sagas, Vol. III 167
'In Praise of the Father' 59-60
Ine, King of Wessex 127-8
Innocent, C.F., author 87-8
Irish 46

Kenneth, King of the Scots 18-19
kingship 15
Knutsdrapa 21-2

land 13-14, 31-2, 34-5, 82, 127-8
Lasrian, Saint 146
Last Poets of Imperial Rome, The
   59-60
laws 126-42; of Aethelbirht 133; of
   Aethelstan 134, 135-6; of Alfred
   the Great 133, 134; of Cnut 141,
   142; of Eadric, King of Kent
   126-7; of Edgar 115-16, 118, 122,
   136-9; of Edmund 38; of Ethel-
   red II, the Redeless 140-1; of
   Hlothhere, King of Kent 126-7; of
   Ine 82, 127-8; of the Northum-
   brian Priests 124-5
Leach, A.F., author 53
learning 44-6, 47-52, 53, 55, 105-7
'Leather Pouches' 38
*Leechdoms, Wortconning and Star-
   craft of Early England* 80, 120,
   139-40
Life of King Alfred 14-15, 47-51,
   53-5, 112-14, 151-2
Life of King Edward the Confessor
   24-6
Life of St Columba 100
Life of St Guthlac 148
Life of St Oswald 19
Llywarch the Aged 62-3

Maelgwn, Western King 11-13
mail coats 155
magic 62, 76, 128-31, 132-3
marriage 36-7
massacre of St Brice's Day 158-9
Matthew of Westminster 96-7
'Mead, the Honey Drink' 42
Medieval English Verse 62
*Medieval Preachers and Medieval
   Preaching* 109-11
Memorials of St Dunstan 115
Mercians 107-8, 148
miracles 28-30, 115, 148
monks, monasteries 44-6, 94-5, 99,
   104-5, 108-9, 112-14, 118-21